Life After Birth Trauma

Life After Birth Trauma

The Road to Recovery

A Project by Jessica Prime

ISBN 978-1-9160686-1-2

Cover and text design by Jen Parker at Fuzzy Flamingo
www.fuzzyflamingo.co.uk

Illustration of mum and baby by Kate Worrall
www.kateprime.co.uk

I would like to dedicate this book to anyone searching for answers or looking to learn.

To my baby girl, Seren, who made me a better, stronger and more determined person, who gives me inspiration, and who I admire and love wholeheartedly.

And to my partner, Matt, who stands by my side, even through the hardest days.

In Support

Jessica Prime is delighted to announce that the Life After Birth Trauma book project is a proud sponsor of The Birth Trauma Association.

The Birth Trauma Association (BTA) is a charity that supports women who suffer birth trauma – a shorthand term for post-traumatic stress disorder (PTSD) after birth.

The Birth Trauma Association provide support, education and awareness to parents and professionals on the topic of birth trauma, and surrounding issues.

www.birthtraumaassociation.org.uk/
www.facebook.com/Birth-Trauma-Association-UK
www.twitter.com/BirthTrauma
The Birth Trauma Association also provide a support group:
www.facebook.com/groups/TheBTA/

With Thanks

With thanks to Jackie Allatson, Certified Birth Trauma Resolution Practitioner, for offering support and care for our co-authors whilst they relived traumatic moments during the writing process.

A warm and grateful thanks to all the authors, who shared deep and personal experiences in order to allow others to heal or learn. I know it was not an easy journey and took great courage and strength. I have admiration and love for you all.

And thanks to you, for supporting the book project and reading with an open mind.

In Loving Memory

In loving memory of the babies who were taken from us too soon.

Claire Wozencroft.

Sienna Maria Strasdin.

Teddy Auger.

Lucie-Mai.

Lee and Christopher Clarke.

Laurina, Lynsey, Lucy, Jamie and Crystal Protheroe.

Baby Lola and Baby Ruby.

Ava Evans.

Brady Telford Lilley.

Baby Chambers 1 and 2.

Contents

Birth Trauma xiii

An introduction to birth trauma and our book project. Why we chose to start the project and why the world needs to pay more attention to birth education.

Our Stories:

Jessica Prime 1
Lisa Norman 15
Dee Mani-Mitchell 25
Elaine Godley 45
Aime Armstrong 56
Emma Louise Hammond 65
Victoria Coupe 77
Lola Lunn 90
Michelle Chambers 104
Chantal Le Moel 116
Alison Ashley 129
Chelle Clarke 137
Sarah Auger 150
David Lilley: Dad's Perspective 158

Positive Birth 172

By Jackie Allatson

Words of Wisdom 189

Words of guidance, love and hope from mums who have already walked a mile in your shoes.

Support 197

Contacts and links if you need extra support.

Birth Trauma

Birth trauma is a definition that covers a range of negative birthing experiences. Those who suffer a traumatic birth may experience post-traumatic stress disorder (PTSD), flashbacks, nightmares, triggers and depression.

According to The Birth Trauma Association, around 30,000 women in the UK experience birth trauma each year. That is a staggering figure, and it doesn't account for those around the world, or those who don't have the support to open up. It also doesn't account for dads, partners or professionals, who can also experience trauma.

There are many factors that can contribute to the experience of birth trauma; usually they include loss of control, the attitudes and behaviours of professionals, a lack of education or information, a loss of dignity, lengthy and exhausting births or quick and painful births, induction and intervention, a lack of pain relief, impersonal treatment, fear of injury or death for mother or baby, poor care and much more. Birth trauma is a complex issue that could often be avoided.

When I had my first child, Seren, I felt an overwhelming disappointment. I had been promised that childbirth was a natural and empowering experience, but the reality for me was far different. After a tough pregnancy and birth, I found myself experiencing symptoms of PTSD. I felt anxious, constantly fearful, depressed and angry. I didn't understand why, so I internalised those feelings and thought the worst of myself. I thought I must be the only person in the whole world who felt that way after birth; and that I must be a terrible mother.

The support network for birth trauma was limited; I hadn't been told about it by my health visitor and no one seemed to be talking about it. I even found that some women who hadn't experienced birth trauma found it hard to empathise or comprehend the situation; some were angered by the topic. This created a lot of shame and guilt.

Triggers meant that I held on to a lot of anxiety; I was in a state of hypervigilance, in constant worry that something bad could happen to my baby. I avoided leaving the house and was overwhelmed with stress if I had to go out with my newborn. Though I eventually learned to work on the anxiety, I still experience triggers years on. The topic of birth is a sensitive one for me; I relate it to pain and distress. I find myself concerned for pregnant women, rather than sharing in their glory. I avoid hospitals and cry when there are birth scenes on the TV. I can't bring myself to have another child, despite us wanting to have a bigger family, and that makes me feel guilty and selfish.

When I finally opened up, I was overwhelmed with support; many women, and some men, opened up to me that they too, had felt traumatised by the birth experience. I realised that what I was experiencing was a much bigger issue than I'd first thought. I eventually learned that the experience had a name; birth trauma. I felt relief sharing my experience with others and finding out that it was actually quite common.

I couldn't fathom that no one seemed to be talking about birth trauma. I had 'secret' messages from women too embarrassed, ashamed or afraid to open up, even to family and friends. I also heard from fathers, who had been witness to traumatic births and had negative experiences and memories. I realised that many people were suffering in silence, and I wanted to change that. I launched the 'Life After Birth Trauma' book project to give those women and men a voice, and to start the conversation.

I was initially worried that the project would create a lot of negative emotion around birth, but that isn't our mission. Positive birth experiences are very possible and can be empowering and beautiful; we want to share our stories to show the world what went wrong for us, we want things to change.

The key to ending birth trauma is education and awareness. Once we start having open conversations about birth, parents can be prepared and empowered.

We hope our stories will inspire positive change; we hope they will create education and awareness. We experienced trauma but we did recover, and we are stronger than ever. These are our stories of overcoming birth trauma.

★★★

"Tell your story.
Shout it. Write it.
Whisper it if you have to.
But tell it.
Some won't understand it.
Some will outright reject it.
But many will
thank you for it.
And then the most
magical thing will happen.
One by one… your tribe will gather.
And you will never feel alone again."

– L.R Knost

Jessica

I have always wanted to be a mother. From an early age, that was the end goal for me. I always wanted to have a big family and imagined being the matriarch to a full and loving family, full to the brim with chaos, fun and laughter. I yearned to have a busy family home, and to be the home that everyone else came to; to be the host. I always thought I would be good at motherhood, and that having my own family would be my happy ending. So, when it happened, but it was unexpected and traumatic, I struggled to recover and to process what I had been through.

I have come to realise that motherhood involves a lot of guilt. Some of it can be motivating and inspires change for the better, but most of it is just time consuming and wasteful. I feel like I have missed out on enjoying the wonders of having a baby, because the time that surrounded the experience was so miserable for me. I wasn't prepared or equipped to deal with the trauma that life threw at me in between having a baby and learning to be a mother.

I think there are many components that constituted to my traumatic birth experience, but fundamentally, I was uneducated and totally unprepared. It has been several years of learning curves, serious changes in who I am, and a whole load of determination and stubbornness to get me to where I am today.

Although I had always wanted a child, and I'd wanted to be a mother for a long time, it happened at a time I least expected and was least prepared for it. I no longer had my own home or a stable job and income. I was technically homeless, in debt, and had only been with my partner for five months when our little surprise happened. Although I had always wanted this, suddenly everything seemed to wrong.

How could I have been so careless, so naïve, so stupid. I was bringing a child into the world, when I could offer no security. What was I thinking? And how could I expect my new partner, Matt, to support me and make this lifelong commitment with me?

I did feel love the for baby, really, I did, but I felt so disappointed in myself.

Pregnancy was tough for me; I know it's tough for so many women and I'm not comparing, but I hated my pregnancy journey. There was no pregnancy radiance or glow to me, it was the sickest I have ever been in my life. My mental and physical health took a massive hit, and I spent most of my time in bed sleeping. I struggled, really struggled, with the changes happening within me, and changes that were also happening in other areas of my personal life. I slept because I was so sick and exhausted, but also, to avoid dealing with the troubles that surrounded me.

I had a grasp on what was happening to my body, and I found it amazing that a little life was growing inside me, but I couldn't envision a happy ending waiting for me. Honestly, I didn't think I even deserved the fairy-tale ending.

Immediately after our first positive test, crisis struck. I was having terrible cramping pains and there had been some bleeding. I was very worried and desperate – I didn't know what to do.

I frantically called medical centre after medical centre, but no one would help me. I wasn't registered in the area, and no one was willing to help until I registered; the only problem was that I was only allowed to register within my catchment area, and no one quite knew what my catchment area was. No one would take me, and no one could recommend a surgery that would be able to.

After calling several surgeries, the local infirmary and the national health helpline, I finally found a medical centre willing to take me, but the registration process would take a few days, and they wouldn't see me or speak to me until the process was complete. I explained my symptoms and asked if I could speak to a doctor just for some reassurance, but it was against protocol, and the receptionist told me, "It sounds like you're losing the baby… But it will still take three days for your registration to go through, and you can't see a doctor until you're registered."

I was desperate and devastated. I had only received the news of pregnancy that day, and already I was being told I might lose the baby.

Matt was also desperate, he could see how sick and upset I was, and he was worried. He also saw how the local medical centres were treating me and he was angry. The safety of our child was at risk, and no one would help us. We rushed to A+E and after a few days of tests and scans, we came away with good news – the baby was healthy, but we were warned to be cautious and to keep a watchful eye on my condition.

Matt and I put together the pieces of what it would be like to be a family; we talked about the possibilities and our worries. We were scared but in it together, we were a team. We developed a sense of 'us' and what that would look like. As we grew closer and changed from partners to 'family', we got some news that would set us back.

It happened accidently; I wasn't feeling myself and asked for some samples to be taken, it wasn't routine, and it was more for peace of mind. But the results showed we had some reason to be worried.

I had tested positive for Group B Strep. What is it? How did this happen? Did I cause this? Could I have prevented this? Could it harm my baby? Am I contagious? So many questions ran through my mind for weeks after my diagnosis – I had never even heard about this infection until now, and now it was too late, because I already had it, and there was a chance that it could harm my baby.

"Don't worry," advised my midwife, "It's very common. I'll send you a leaflet." A few days later, I received a basic leaflet that told me I had tested positive for Group B Strep, which is a bacterial infection, but that my baby would receive antibiotics during birth and that it was extremely common. I needed to know more. I needed to know what was wrong with me. I researched as much as I could. It wasn't just about knowing the facts and stats, I needed to understand why and how this had happened.

One in four mothers have Group B Strep during pregnancy; it is very common and generally most babies that come into contact with the bacteria are totally unaffected. But those babies that are affected are at the risk of terrible illnesses including sepsis, pneumonia, meningitis and even death.

This is an issue that effects 25% of women. On average, one baby a week dies from GBS infection and one baby a week survives with long-term disability. I couldn't believe that I had never heard of it.

I felt like a failure, before it had even started. All I had to do was grow a healthy baby inside me, and I couldn't even do that. I couldn't understand why an infection inside my body might cause serious harm to my baby. It doesn't make sense that the same place that grows and nurtures her, could also hurt her.

The rest of the pregnancy developed mostly normally; the baby grew slower than expected, but everything was being monitored and I was expecting antibiotics during labour to protect the baby from the infection. It was scary, but hopeful.

When I asked friends and mothers for advice, they reassured me, "Birth is the most natural thing in the world. You'll be fine."

At the time, I didn't know you could refuse an induction or that there could be implications, so when my consultant told me I would be induced the following morning, I didn't question her.

On the day of my induction I was oddly calm on the surface, but my mind and anxiety ran wild inside. It's a strange feeling to know that you are going to give birth today. I'm going to have a baby. Today, I'll become a mother.

The hormone used to induce labour was inserted and the labour progressed quickly. We would later discover that I was hypersensitive to the hormone, which meant I had no breaks or relief from the contractions. I was in constant agony but made to feel as if I was being dramatic.

The midwife did what we could, and I don't blame her for my experience, but she was overwhelmed and would often leave me in the care of my partner. Matt did everything he could to comfort me, but he's not medically trained, so we were often left alone and terrified with a total lack of experience, and he felt helpless. Often, there were no midwives available when we called for help.

As time went by, the pain of the contractions became unbearable. Almost immediately after the induction I was in so much pain that I couldn't even walk. Due to the sensitivity and pace of my labour, contractions came and went with barely a break in between. "Poor you", the midwife would say.

Time felt so quick and so slow at the same time. Because I wasn't coping, the midwife recommended pethidine. "It won't stop the pain," she explained, "but it will take the edge off." Until now I had been surviving with only paracetamol and co-codamol, so I was desperate for anything that would help. I just wanted some relief, but it didn't help, and I later wished I had never agreed. Pethidine made me feel like I was paralysed but totally conscious. As I laid in agony, I tried to muster the energy to tell them it wasn't working but I couldn't move or speak. I could hear them comment on how peaceful I looked, and how it must be doing good, but my insides felt like they were being ripped apart whilst I laid there lifeless. I felt trapped in my mind. I was screaming "HELP ME!", but no sound came out.

I remember thinking the current contraction was the worst feeling in the world, and not being sure I could handle it, then the next one would come, ten times worse, and I'd wish for the easier one before. Over and over again. They never seemed to end, and I couldn't control my cries for help.

Despite the hypersensitivity, labour lasted hours.

I can't explain the level of pain and fear I experienced on the way to my delivery room. The baby was coming, and so far, I'd had no relief. I wasn't able to walk. The pain was unreal, and I remember thinking I was going to die. I couldn't possibly imagine enduring any more, and when I heard the agonising screams of other ladies on the ward, I remember silently accepting that this would be the place that I would die. But I wasn't ready; I didn't want to die.

Now I understand it was adrenaline that caused the women to scream, but at the time, I felt like I was in a place of torture and pain. "I can't!" I pleaded with the midwife as she laid me on the bed. "It's too much", I cried. She passed me the gas and air. Finally, some relief.

At this point, I really should have been put on an intravenous drop to begin treating and protecting my baby. After my partner had mentioned it several times, the midwife proceeded to do so. "Oh shit! I forgot!" She said. But it was too late, the baby was very much on her way, so antibiotics were abandoned.

The easiest way for me to describe gas and air is that I felt out-of-body. I felt like I was floating, and occasionally aware of my pain and surroundings. It helped me to focus and calm down. I could hear chatting in the room. I could feel Matt stroking my head and telling me, "You're doing great." Every now and then I'd feel my body contract and push naturally. As things progressed and I was calmer, I was aware of what those in the room were telling me, and I was slow and weak, but able to eventually communicate calmly. "On the next contraction I need you to push," said the health practitioner. She guided me through the contractions and helped me to focus on what was happening. As I became more alert, I was aware there were many people in the room now. A midwife held my right foot and leg up, a practitioner supported my left foot and leg and held my left hand, Matt held my right hand and stroked my head, and a doctor sat between my legs, looking to see what was happening. Other people came and went, occasionally telling me things that I would agree to, but I can't remember what.

I was always told that birth was the most natural thing in the world. When I questioned or wanted to know more, people would tell me, "Just trust yourself. Your body will know what to do. After all, women have been doing this for thousands of years." That is probably the worst advice I've ever been given about birth, and yet, you'll find that it's common. The problem with this advice is that it doesn't take into consideration that sometimes the body doesn't know what to do, that the mother may not be coping and that there are other factors involved. It doesn't allow the mother to prepare for options or to be educated about the facts. My body didn't know what to do, and if it did, it was too exhausted to do it. By the time it came to give birth, I was spent. I couldn't give anymore.

"The baby is struggling, she's distressed." I heard the doctor tell me.

"Help me, please!" I begged him.

The doctor explained what needed to be done, but I was too exhausted and terrified to completely understand. I was opened up surgically with scissors; I remember feeling him cutting away at me, I remember feeling the scissors tear my muscle.

A ventouse cup was placed inside me, and onto the baby's head, to assist. I pushed a few more times with all my might, screaming as my adrenaline surged, and my baby was born.

She was taken to the side to be checked over having gone into distress. I took a few moments to process what had happened, but then I wept. "I did it!" I told Matt, as I was overcome with relief. It was finally over.

By the time they placed the baby on my chest, I was more alert. I could see I was covered in blood. My blood covered the bed, bedding, floor, medical trolley and doctor. I sat in disbelief as the doctor stitched me back up. There was so much blood, it was everywhere.

I was never told much about the long-term effects of having an episiotomy or being cut open during birth. Professionals always said not to worry too much, that it would only happen if it absolutely had to, but that it would heal, and the vagina would 'bounce back'. It doesn't. No one seems to talk openly about this, but had I known the long-term effects, I would have asked for other options. Though I did heal well physically, I felt the pain of the stitches for years, and even now, occasionally the scar tissue is sore and tender to touch; it also meant our sex life had to adapt. Nothing 'bounced back'.

I cautiously touched the baby that had been placed on my chest; I couldn't quite believe she was mine. 'What am I going to do with a baby?' I thought; I was totally in over my head. I waited for instructions, hoping someone would pass me a manual, or tell me what I needed to do next. No such luck.

The days that followed my birth were some of the most lonely I've ever experienced. Matt wasn't allowed to stay with us at the hospital, as there was an outdated policy in place that disallowed men after visiting hours, so not long after I had given birth, we were told not to get too comfortable. The midwife pointed at Matt, "You will have to leave." We were dumbfounded and panicked. Our lives had just changed forever, and now Matt was being sent away.

I was left alone with our newborn, totally exhausted, still covered in my own blood and totally out of my depth. I remember spending the night awake, counting down the hours until we saw him again. I was exhausted, but too frightened to sleep. The baby slept in my arms, and I watched her. All night. I pushed a buzzer when she cried; I had no idea what I was doing.

I didn't sleep for days after. I felt abandoned.

The second night things took a turn for the worse, and my worst nightmares were realised. The baby was acting strange. She was agitated, barely woke, barely ate and turned a yellow colour. The midwife on duty was concerned and immediately called for a doctor. After several blood tests, and a lot of tears, it was agreed that the baby had caught an infection, but they didn't know what it was.

I knew; it was me.

I'd passed on my infection.

It was all my fault.

I was told the baby would need to undergo further testing, and I was led to the Special Care Baby Unit (SCBU). Bewildered, confused, upset and still with no sleep, I asked the midwife if I could call Matt to tell him what had happened. "No. Tell him tomorrow", she told me.

As they placed my baby on to the medical table, I was told to be prepared. "This will be too upsetting", said a kind nurse.

"Come with me and wait in the other room." Thankfully, finally, I had met a nurse who showed me empathy. She comforted me and told me she would do everything she could to help. They needed to extract fluids from my baby's spine for testing; the screams from the other room were unbearable; I couldn't control my reaction. My worried tears had now become hysterical cries.

Even now, years on, I can still hear those screams, and every time, I get that torn up feeling in my stomach when I hear it. I don't think it will ever leave me.

I couldn't believe the lack of compassion from the midwife on duty, so called my partner anyway. It was four in the morning and I called him to explain what was happening. The baby was undergoing a lumbar puncture; I could hear her screams from the waiting room they had taken me to, and I was distraught. I begged him to come back to the hospital, I simply couldn't do this alone.

The midwives told me that he would not be allowed to come into the ward, or stay, I kept hearing 'policy, policy, policy' but I didn't care about their outdated policy, our child was sick, why shouldn't her dad be there too? I was hysterical with upset; I couldn't understand their lack of empathy or why they were being so difficult and offering no help or support, they just kept repeating their policy. I cried so hard I struggled for air. Policy or not, I couldn't understand how or why they expected me to deal with this alone. The kind nurse who had looked after me before promised she would do her best to help.

We were eventually given a private side room, and told to await results from the tests, however the lumbar puncture had failed, and we would have to re-sit that tomorrow.

The baby was a very sad sight. By now, she too had an intravenous drip inserted into her tiny hand, and the ventouse cup had left a huge bruise which is now a scar. She was so tiny and fragile; we were heartbroken, and I blamed myself for her sickness. After all, I was the one with Group B Strep and I wondered what I could have done to have prevented this. I wondered if Matt blamed me too.

Attending the lumbar puncture the next day, I cried before it had even begun. I knew what to expect, and I couldn't bear to think of the screams that were about to come. Matt told me to calm down, but by the time the baby was screaming, he was in tears too. We couldn't bear the sound of our child in pain, and when the doctors came to tell us this second time had failed too, we were furious and declined any further punctures. "We're not exactly sure what the infection is," they explained, "but we don't think it's meningitis." We left with no more knowledge or insight than before, the word 'meningitis' ringing in our ears.

On the third night, I was so exhausted and still hadn't slept. I kept passing out. I was faint and dizzy, and unable to stay awake. Something wasn't right. The midwives were dismissive and told me I was fine, but after my persistence and demanding blood tests, results showed that my iron levels had depleted. I was prescribed iron. But the good news was that Matt was allowed to stay with us, at least for now.

There were a few really kind midwives who could tell I was struggling and wanted to help, they tried to convince senior staff members and board members to allow Matt to stay, but it was a battle we would fight throughout our time at the hospital, and eventually lose.

By the fourth night I was experiencing panic attacks worse than anything I've ever experienced. During the night, I would wake up screaming, startling myself, as well as Matt. I would sweat and cry in my sleep. My dreams mirrored my experience of labour, and I'd cry out for help. I'd feel paralysed again and lunge out for comfort. My heart would beat so hard, and the palpitations would hurt. Every day we would wonder and worry about what was happening to our child, and if Matt would be allowed to stay, or if he would be forced to leave us again.

After a few nights, Matt was asked to leave again, and when I cried and pleaded with the head midwife to reconsider, she asked, "How do you expect to cope at home? You can't even cope here, with our help." I wondered what help she had been referring to. Matt left, and we were alone again.

Parenthood is not a feminine issue; I couldn't fathom why fathers were treated like day guests. I'll always remember a young lady who I had seen on the ward. She, like me, was exhausted. I felt empathy for her, but never spoke to her. One night she was so exhausted she dropped her baby on to the hard hospital floor. Her sobs echoed into my cubicle, and I heard her whisper repeatedly, "I'm so sorry". The midwife told me, "Be careful you don't drop your baby, like that mother did", pointing at the cubicle next to mine. I felt so sorry for her, I wanted to reach out and offer support, but I wasn't in any position to help anyone else. I think I'll always regret that I didn't reach out to her. I couldn't imagine all this chaos if they just allowed dads to stay and help.

One thing that I learned during this experience is that our little girl is a fighter. It was a long eight days, but we were finally discharged; she had fought off the infection.

We left the hospital different people; feeling beaten but relieved. The baby had scars, but she was strong.

We named her Seren Mai, or as her late great-grandmother called her, 'Star of May'.

We later learned that previously that year, the hospital had undergone inspections and had been deemed 'unfit for purpose' and 'a poor environment for women' by experts. In 2018 it was given a £25m grant, and I cried when I found out. I really truly hope that no one else has to experience what we went through or be treated the way we were. My mental health suffered for years after.

Leaving the hospital, it felt like our troubles were over. It was scary leaving as new parents, but it felt as if the bad days were behind us. I had always wanted to be a mother; I had dreams of a big family, but I don't think I'll ever be brave enough to try for another child. I am wiser and stronger for what I went through, but not braver.

What Went Wrong?

I feel a lot of resentment for my birthing experience, but mostly I feel sad that no one prepared me for what could happen or spoke honestly. I understand that pregnancy and birth is scary, especially for a first-time mum, but how can we ever expect women to feel prepared and empowered, if they don't understand that things can and do go wrong. My healthcare professionals should have shown more empathy and I should have been more prepared for the realities of birth. I use my experience to advocate and promote good health and awareness. I don't want women to feel afraid like I did, and still do sometimes, I want them to know they deserve better, to educate themselves and to be empowered. And I dream of the day that dads are allowed to stay with their new family at hospital, to support, to bond, and to be a family. Imagine how differently my story (and many more) could have been if we'd been allowed to stay together as a family.

★★★

Jessica Prime is a best-selling author and advocate, and founder of Child Author Project.

Born in South Wales, UK, Jessica Prime is a mother to Seren, fiancée to Matthew and a trustee for Faye Knowles

Chapman Foundation, campaigning to lower the age for cervical screening and advocating for cervical health awareness and education.

Jessica has been writing poetry, stories and content from a young age, first published in 2001, in a children's poetry collection.

Jessica became a best-selling author in 2018 when she shared her experience of birth trauma with Mums in Business Association in Mumpreneur on Fire 3 book.

Through years of mental health struggles, a traumatic birth and a series of infections, Jessica writes about real life struggles and exposes the truth of her experiences. An advocate for mental health and women's health issues, Jessica explores raw, real life issues in an attempt to create awareness, end stigma and create empowerment.

www.jessicaprime.co.uk
www.childauthorproject.com

Lisa

Birth trauma is so hard to talk about, why is that? I'm sure there are many correct answers to this question but here is my opinion; It relates to mental health (which is still a little bit of a taboo subject). With the pressures from society that you need to be seen as the good mother that has her head together, we ignore the trauma and try and bury it so deep so that we can get on with day to day living. It comes back though in different ways and keeps nibbling away at the edges of your life until you deal with it or break.

Whatever your opinion, I strongly believe it's a topic that needs to be discussed so I am very grateful for the opportunity that Jessica gave me to be part of this book. My birth trauma story may be hard for some of you to read so I will assure you at the beginning that there's a happy ending!

In May 2016 I took a pregnancy test that came back negative, but I just knew it couldn't be right. I booked in to see my doctor and they also did a test that came back negative, so I was sent for a blood test. I received a call a few days later congratulating me on my pregnancy. Me and my husband were stunned and happy with the news. We were looking forward to the next chapter in our lives.

At my 12-week scan I was told I had PAAP-A. The nurse wasn't worried about this development but did explain that it meant there was a protein deficiency in the placenta so for the last 10 weeks of my pregnancy I would get extra scans just to check that my baby was growing properly. These scans were routine and nothing to worry about. The 20-week scan appointment soon came around and I won the argument with my husband about finding out the sex of the baby. We were expecting a boy! Everything looked normal and the sonographer was happy with our son's progress.

At 23 weeks I was signed off from work, my son was sat so low that there was an immense amount of pressure on my hips and lower spine. I wasn't comfortable lying, sitting or standing. I attended several antenatal classes to help strengthen and stretch my muscles to try and get some relief. I also tried acupuncture. Nothing gave me long term relief though and by 23 weeks I was so uncomfortable that I couldn't face going into the office.

My 30-week scan came around quickly and I couldn't wait to see the grainy black, white and grey image of my son on the monitor. I was in a lot of pain now and this scan was something I was really looking forward to. My husband and I set off early for the hospital knowing that parking could be an issue. We weren't let down either as that prized parking space was nowhere to be found. My husband dropped me off at the maternity unit doors so that I could go into the scan appointment and be on time.

I went in and sat down. My bladder was uncomfortably full, so I was pleased to see that they were running pretty much to time. I was soon called in. I explained that my husband was trying to find a parking space so might join us at some point. The sonographer started the scan, she pointed out my baby's head, spine, arms and legs. Then she asked me to check if my husband had been in contact. He hadn't. She made a few taps on the keyboard in front of her and said that she was going to tell security she was giving permission for him to park in the 10-minute bay at the front of the maternity unit. She didn't give me chance to respond and quickly left me alone in the room.

I rang my husband and explained what the sonographer was doing. He works for the emergency services so was a little reluctant to park in the emergency bay but agreed and soon joined me. As soon as he sat down the sonographer restarted the scan and told us that there was something wrong with our son. She pointed out a build-up of fluid on his tummy that shouldn't be there. We later found out this was called Hydrops Fetalis and if that fluid reached his heart and lungs he would drown. She also told us that his heart rate was far too high. We later found out this condition is called Supraventricular Tachycardia or SVT for short.

The sonographer went on to explain that she had already sent the scan up to the doctors to assess. She was going to leave us for a few minutes to find out what the doctors' thought was the best course of action. Me and my husband were left alone in a private waiting room, we both felt numb and I was grateful for the hug he gave me. The sonographer was back and told us that I was going up for surgery right now!

Tears were streaming down my face as I waddled through the waiting area that was full of expectant mums waiting for their scans. I turned my head away as I didn't want them to see how upset I was. The sonographer was in a big hurry and I couldn't keep up. She secured a lift and once inside my husband took me into a much-needed big bear hug. He later told me I looked like I needed it but also the sonographer had started to cry, and he wanted to protect me from seeing her upset.

I was met by a nurse when the lift doors opened, and I was directed to a private room. My tears suddenly stopped, and I somehow pulled myself together. I was stripped of my clothes and jewellery, I had a catheter put in, I was jabbed with all sorts of needles and I was asked the same set of questions by three different people. I was ready for surgery.

My husband was taken off to get a set of theatre scrubs on. A nurse told him that our baby was really poorly, and the theatre team didn't think he was likely to survive delivery. Statistically only 20% of babies with Hydrops survive delivery and only 10% survive beyond delivery. Meanwhile I was in theatre having an epidural. The nurse with me was so lovely. He had a dry sense of humour that amazingly made me smile.

There was a little confusion as to whether I was to stay awake or be put to sleep for the procedure. The registrar ruled that she was happy for me to stay awake, I am a little grateful for the confusion as I got to take the anti-sickness medication they give you if they put you under anaesthetic. Once they were happy, I had no feeling in the lower half of my body they began performing the caesarean section. I was pre-warned that I would feel a strange sensation as they pushed my baby out of the incision. They weren't kidding! I yelped out at suddenly being able to feel the pressure of them pushing down. They checked I was ok, and I quickly assured them I was fine, just not prepared for how it would feel.

From my appointment time to my son's delivery into the world it was 2 hours and 2 minutes. We were greeted with silence though. There was no baby cry. The theatre team were so well versed in what they were doing that they didn't need to communicate to each other verbally. The suspension was too much for me, I was afraid to distract the team from their tasks in hand, so I asked my husband to peek around the dividing sheet going across my body. He isn't squeamish so was happy to take a look. He reported back that he couldn't see anything. We waited and wittered on about anything that popped into our heads this helped to distract me from what was actually happening.

An incubator was wheeled next to me and we were allowed to look at our son for a minute before they had to rush him up to the neonatal unit. I thought I loved my son when he was a bump but actually seeing him brought a whole new intensity to that feeling of love. The minute was over far too quickly.

We were pushed for a name and my husband supplied the last name we had discussed Neil Eric Norman, named after both his grandads. Once the team had a name, they whisked our son off to the Neonatal Intensive Care Unit (NICU) so they could work on stabilising him. His heart rate was recorded at 320 beats per minute, the staff had never seen a heart rate so high.

I was stitched up by the registrar and sent to recovery. For the rest of the day I had my own room. The nurses kept coming with updates but essentially there was no change. After about 4 hours my husband and Mum were allowed to go and see Neil. I quickly handed over my phone with strict instructions to take pictures. I was briefly left on my own to reflect on what had happened. I wasn't alone for long as my observations were due, so a nurse distracted me from the burdening thoughts swirling round in my mind. Soon my husband and Mum were back, and I had a few pictures to look through.

My little boy was so swollen from the fluid that he almost looked like a tiny but plump newborn. His small body was now covered in wires and a breathing tube was going down to his lungs to help him breathe. Over the next few weeks we were told daily that they didn't know if he was going to survive. The fluid started to drain from his limbs making his arms and legs very skinny. He was surviving on TPN (Total Parent Nutrition) as he couldn't tolerate my milk. He was on so much medication; none of which was getting his SVT heart condition under control. The doctors were starting to talk to us about heart failure being a real possibility. Then, Neil's heart stayed in SVT for a full 24 hours with absolutely no break. A short episode to a grown adult is the equivalent of them running a marathon. The doctors decided it was time for Neil to move to a more specialist hospital.

I was so upset. This hospital was further away and the fact

that he needed that extra level of care made me so anxious. The papers were filed, the bed arranged, and the transportation booked. On route to Alder Hey Children's Hospital my son's bed was taken. He was diverted to Liverpool Women's Hospital where the Alder Hey doctors would go and see him. It turned out to be the best thing that happened. Within 12 hours of Neil being at Liverpool Women's the cardiologist had Neil's SVT under control. It was amazing! Neil went from strength to strength and 2 days before Christmas Royal Preston Hospital agreed that they could take Neil back under their care.

Neil went from strength to strength and after 73 days on the neonatal unit we were finally allowed home. It took the entire day to be discharged as the pharmacist had to order in specialist medication. At 8pm we finally walked through the front door. We had no time to stop and think though as I needed to unpack the medication and sort out his next bottle and all the medication that was due in that bottle. I was overwhelmed by the amount of medicine and my husband had to put it away, so it didn't look as daunting.

The neonatal home visit team came out every day to check we were doing ok and introduced us to Marie, an amazing community nurse, who would be taking over from them (and still has Neil under her care for which I am incredibly grateful). On the fourth day at home our world fell apart. My husband had made me a cup of tea and took over feeding Neil his bottle so I could relax for 5 minutes. Suddenly my husband was really alarmed and telling me that our son wasn't breathing, I looked over and thought he was just snoozing after his bottle. His tiny body had gone lifeless though and he very quickly turned blue. My husband quickly rushed to put Neil on a firm surface and began performing CPR. Thankfully my husband's job means that he regularly gets refresher training on first aid and CPR. I dialled 999 and explained what was happening.

An emergency responder and two ambulances turned onto our street just as Neil let out a whimper. My husband had done it and managed to revive our little baby boy. We were blue lighted back to the hospital where my son spent a further week battling with bronchiolitis. We have never had to resuscitate him again, but it wouldn't be the last emergency visit to the children's ward.

Come April, it was time for me to start thinking about returning to work. I just couldn't do it. We made the tough decision that I would take a huge pay cut and have a further 6 months off. I became increasingly aware that my mental health had been affected by so many traumatic events, starting back with my son's birth. I was worried about going to my doctor. What would they say? Would I be told off for wasting their time? Would they tell me to get out and be grateful that my son was alive and doing reasonably well? My doctor was really understanding and talked me through a few different options. I opted for talking therapy.

I was soon under the care of an amazing therapist called Emily. She quickly diagnosed me with Post Traumatic Stress Disorder (PTSD) and anxiety. She talked over a few options with me and I decided that Cognitive Behavioural Therapy (CBT) was the way to go. The NHS allocate 6 sessions per patient; after that the therapist has to put a good case together for more sessions to be approved.

I returned to work and on my third full day back my manager asked how I was doing. That simple question had me in floods of tears, I wasn't coping well at all. I felt I had been asked so many times about Neil's birth that I was suffocating. I was heading to a therapy session so I said I would talk it through and see if there were any suggestions that I could pass on to my manager the next day. I ended up doing a phased return to work and slowly built my hours back up to full time.

I worked hard in all my therapy sessions. I did the homework I was set and because Emily had created such a safe space for me to open up and talk, I took full advantage of the precious sessions I was offered. In the end I had 23 sessions. Some were a lot tougher than others to get through. Part of the work we did was to relive the memories, it was scary to do this. Emily had talked to me in one session to see if it was something that I would like to try as the success from this exercise can be really beneficial. I agreed that in the next session we could give it a go. Before going into that next appointment, I felt physically sick. I knew the work we were going to do would be beneficial to me but the thought of looking more deeply into some of those memories filled me with dread.

In that moment I realised I was always going to feel like this and that the reason I threw myself wholeheartedly into CBT was to get more control over this feeling. I went in and Emily talked me through the session plan again and checked I still wanted to go ahead. I did. The session was emotionally draining, and I felt completely and utterly exhausted by the end of it. I also felt a huge relief. Before when these memories surfaced, they gripped me with terror and fear. I felt frozen and unable to catch my breath. Now I had reprocessed the memory with fresh eyes, and I had updated the memory with new information that wasn't available to me at the moment of living those experiences.

As time went on, I was able to continue to update the trauma experience with new information and get to a point where I was comfortable with the memories when they decided to come to the forefront of my mind. I'm so grateful that I had a therapist who was willing to put the time and effort into me and help me as much as she did.

A year on and I still use the tools and techniques I was taught. I also made a self-care plan with Emily so that if I ever felt overwhelmed, I would have a point of reference to help myself get back on track. It's certainly not an easy process but the hardest thing was admitting that I needed help and then seeking that help out.

Neil is thriving as well. We have recently celebrated him getting his final discharge from the neonatal unit and going a full year without needing a hospital admission. He still has SVT and the intubation at birth scarred his lungs, so he also has Chronic Lung Disease. He's getting bigger and stronger everyday though and we're so proud of the fight he has for life. He is such a happy little boy who is always laughing and smiling.

I'm incredibly grateful to the staff at both Royal Preston Hospital and Liverpool Women's Hospital for saving my son's life on multiple occasions and the care they gave him.

★★★

Lisa lives in Lancashire with her husband, son and German Shepherd. In April 2020 Lisa will be welcoming a new baby into the family. Lisa created Presents For Preemies to help family and friends choose thoughtful and useful gifts for premature babies. The blog has been very popular in helping new parents of premature babies understand the new world they have been thrown into. The blog has also attracted some amazing people offering helpful knowledge and ideas as well as some very brave mums who have shared their preemie stories.

Lisa has set up two Facebook support groups, one for parents of premature babies. The other is for family and friends as there are currently no support groups for them out there.

To find out more you can find Lisa:

Website:

www.presentsforpreemies.co.uk
Facebook:
www.facebook.com/PresentsForPreemies
www.facebook.com/groups/PreemieSupportCommunityUK
www.facebook.com/groups/PreemieParentCommunityUK
Instagram:
www.instagram.com/presents_for_preemies

Dee

It was August 2005; I had just finished working 3 months in Greece and had earnt enough money in those 3 months to be able to comfortably take a year off. I left the UK in 2002 when I decided to start a new life in Tenerife, after a few months earning pennies working in bars I got into sales in the vacation industry, I was an exceptionally good closer, I still am now. My job took me to wherever I wanted to go in the world, I was living the dream financially and career wise, however my personal life was less to be desired. I was in a very volatile relationship at the time, with a narcissist alcoholic. Looking back now I cringe at the fact that I was with this person for so long, 7 years in total, the only good thing to come out of that relationship was my 2 children!

So, after Greece, we decided to take a month vacation in Finland, where my partner was from, in a beautiful summer house in the middle of the forest next to a stunning lake. It was peaceful and stress free and just what I needed after 3 months working 15 hours a day, 7 days a week! I remember feeling so exhausted, I put it down to the fact that I was just physically and mentally drained, not only from the long work hours but also from the detrimental relationship I was in. After Finland, we moved to Lanzarote, the plan was to chill for 6 months and then move to Thailand where I could continue my work with the same company I worked for in Greece. A few days after being in Lanzarote I didn't feel right at all, dizzy, sick and constantly tired. After a month doing nothing in Finland, this made me suspicious and I had a feeling that this tiredness was down to pregnancy. After doing a test my fears were confirmed.

I say fears because I was never the maternal type, I grew up around babies with my elder sisters' kids and I felt I didn't need kids to complete my life, I was too career focused. Not only that, I especially didn't want to be starting a family with the person I was with. On the face of it, it's easy to ask why I didn't leave and why I endured such a toxic relationship, I still to this day can't answer that question, I was super strong in my business life, but I was weak in my personal life!

I was 6 weeks pregnant. My partner was ecstatic and promised me he would change his ways, foolishly I believed him. I had my first scan about a month after I did that test and as soon as I saw that image I instantly fell in love, any doubts just disappeared. My partner was still the same, he had no intention of changing, in the back of my mind I knew that with or without him I would cope just fine.

My first trimester was horrendous, luckily, I wasn't working. I was continuously either feeling sick or actually being sick, whoever named it morning sickness were having an absolute laugh, it was morning, noon and night for me. I could hardly eat anything, but the baby was growing at a normal rate, that was all that mattered. My relationship was draining, I hardly ever saw my partner which actually suited me just fine, he was either out drinking or asleep, he didn't care I was feeling so rough and never helped me with daily chores.

I used to smoke and drink (not heavily just socially) before I got pregnant as soon as I tested positive, I immediately quit, however I wasn't really looking after myself in terms of nutrition and I knew that it was affecting my unborn child, I was just in a bad place mentally, I felt depressed from my situation, I knew that I should've kicked my partner out but I just had a nagging voice in the back of my head telling me that being a single parent would be harder than living with a useless piece of shit. Obviously, I was trying to kid myself.

After around 4 months I started getting very bad pains, I kept going to the doctor who just kept telling me it was to be expected with pregnancy. My Spanish wasn't so great at the time and I was in a state hospital, so they didn't need to speak to me in English and rightfully so, I was the one living in Lanzarote I should've adapted the language. This is when I needed to rely on my partner, he was fluent in Spanish and he did make the effort to come with me to all appointments so he could translate, although I'm pretty sure when he was translating he was only telling me what I wanted to hear, he just had no enthusiasm, although he claimed he wanted nothing more than to be a father, I'm pretty sure at these appointments all he was thinking about was which bar he would be going to as soon as he dropped me off.

I hated being pregnant, sickness, tiredness and in extreme pain. I had no family around they were all back in the UK and I hardly had many friends, as soon as we moved to Lanzarote I found out I was pregnant, so it was difficult for me to go out and socialise and meet new people as all I wanted to do was curl up in a ball at home and hope that these awful pregnancy symptoms would soon pass. They didn't pass they just became more intense; I was still being sick throughout the whole gestation.

I gave my partner an ultimatum, either he had to stop drinking or he had to move out, he agreed to get help and he was prescribed Antabus tablets, which basically are a drug and if you drink alcohol on them, they can cause heart failure. The idea is that they act as a deterrent to drink. I was pleased with this outcome, because when he wasn't drinking, he was actually a decent human to be around, having kids was all he ever wanted, and he was doing this for his son. We found out the sex at the last scan, it didn't matter to me either way whether if it was a boy or a girl, but now we knew it was a boy choosing a name was probably the most exciting part of the whole pregnancy. I chose 2 – Kai and Tyler, I would decide which one when he was born.

One night when I was around 6 months pregnant, we went out for a nice meal, I remember it well because we were actually getting on great, no alcohol was involved, he was working and coming straight home and the sickness wasn't as bad as it was the previous months, I was starting to look pregnant, up until then, I just looked a bit fat and nobody even noticed I was actually pregnant. I was proud of my baby bump and actually happy for the first time in a long time with my relationship. During the meal I had a very intense pain, I went to the bathroom and noticed that I was bleeding, it wasn't just spots, it was clots. I was so upset I thought I was losing my baby; we left the restaurant and went straight to the hospital.

Waiting around in hospital for hours, nobody seemed to care, I kept pleading to let me see a doctor quickly as I could feel myself still bleeding and in incredible pain. I had to sit and wait in a wheelchair. I eventually got seen and they refused to let my partner come in with me, I explained that my Spanish wasn't so great, and I needed him to translate but the nurses just kept sniggering at me. They put me on a bed with my legs in those stirrup things, I was so scared thinking what on earth are they going to be doing with me, I had read that you shouldn't have internal examinations when so far pregnant and I was confused as to why they weren't doing an ultrasound to check the heartbeat, but I kept being told to be quiet, I felt like a naughty schoolgirl being told off! The doctor eventually came and gave me an internal examination, it felt so painful, I remember just laying there crying. I just wanted to know if my baby was still alive!

The doctor had explained that the next 48 hours were critical and that I could lose the baby, they wouldn't give any other information, they didn't even seem too bothered about keeping the baby alive, I'm sure it was because I couldn't speak Spanish, they saw me as not worthy of any kind of explanation, go home and rest was all I was told and I wasn't allowed to move around, I had to stay in bed with my legs elevated. I couldn't understand why I needed to be elevated it wasn't as if the baby could drop out with gravity!

When we got home, my partner had given me some long speech about how he was stressed and needed a drink, the tablets he was on only lasted 24 hours, so if he didn't take one on that evening he could drink without having the heart failure. I begged him not to as I needed him there with me, I was stressed too! The past few weeks when he was on this medication were the best in a very long time and it was breaking my heart that he was being so selfish. With disregard for my feelings, he went out and didn't return until 3 days later! Those 3 days were hell, we had no food in the house, and I was bedridden, still bleeding and still in pain. I kept trying to call him, but his phone was off. I managed to drag myself to the shop, I needed to eat. On the way I had convinced myself that my baby had died, I hadn't felt him move for a good while and up until then he was pretty active. At the shop filled with dread and sadness, I bought a bottle of wine and a pack of cigarettes.

Back at home, I sat and sobbed, and I finished the bottle, I barely smoked any as they were making me heave as I hadn't smoked for so long. I was incredibly sad with the whole situation, I felt alone and desperate for attention, eventually I passed out from the wine and tiredness. When I woke up, the pain had gone, and the bleeding had stopped. In my mind I believed that my baby had died, I didn't think there was any other explanation especially after downing a bottle of wine, I felt guilty and distraught. What was I thinking! I just lay there all by myself, feeling low, empty and useless.

I was scared to go to the hospital, but I knew I had to, I was playing visions in my head of me having to give birth to my dead baby, how else would they get him out? I eventually picked up the courage and went to the hospital. This time I had a lovely nurse who did actually speak English to me, I think it was only because she could see how sad and tearful I was. She did an ultrasound and showed me my baby on the screen, he was still alive and his heartbeat was very strong, the doctor that came in couldn't explain why I was bleeding or why I was in pain, to be honest at that point I didn't care, I was just so relieved.

I went home and my partner had just got home, he was absolutely paralytic and passed straight out on the sofa. I looked at him in disgust, he had no idea what I had been through emotionally whilst he was out enjoying himself. I decided I needed to be with my family, and I packed my things and went straight to the airport. I managed to get a flight on standby back to the UK and went straight to my parents' house. I didn't want to have my baby in Lanzarote, I felt much more comfortable being in an English-speaking hospital and having my loved ones around to support me. My mom welcomed me in with open arms, she desperately missed me being abroad.

After a week, my partner had turned up on the doorstep. He had tried to call me several times but I just kept ignoring him, I soon discovered that he had called my mom and she told him I was there and invited him to come over, I was furious at my mom, I felt betrayed, especially after I told her what was happening, she told me I needed him around and that being a single mom would be very hard, she believed he could change, however deep down I knew he never would! The week I was alone, I felt content and my pregnancy felt good, as soon as he came back, I could feel the stress levels rising and the sickness came back. I'm not sure if the sickness I had practically through my whole pregnancy was actual "morning" sickness or whether it was all stress related, the only time during my pregnancy I wasn't sick was when he was on the medication or when he wasn't around when I was in the UK, which lead me to believe it quite possibly was stress. He was still drinking, not on a massive level, but he still was, everybody thought he was lovely, the doting partner and father to be, he manipulated everyone with his charm. I just felt hatred towards him as he wasn't interested in anything to do with the pregnancy or me.

I registered with a hospital, had a scan and was told the baby was doing well but the midwife wasn't too happy with the way my placenta looked so she called a doctor for an opinion. The ultrasound seemed to last forever, the doctor and midwife were both very quiet. The doctor had explained that there was indeed an issue, but it was difficult to ascertain what it was as they couldn't see with the position that the baby was lying in. I was just told to go back weekly to keep an eye on things and once again to rest. A few days after that appointment I was back in extreme pain, so I went to the emergency unit. The doctor on duty asked me if it was my first pregnancy, which of course it was, he told me to go home and that these pains were normal. He belittled me because it was my first and I was inexperienced. I asked for an ultrasound, but he refused, he didn't need to hear the heartbeat as baby was moving around, even after mentioning the placenta issues, I was still told to go home.

A few days later, the pain became more intense, so bad that I couldn't even stand, once again I took myself to the hospital, they hooked me up to a monitor and confirmed that they were contractions. As I was only 34 weeks pregnant, they told me they were Braxton Hicks and not the "real deal". I was confused because I had read that these preparation contractions are rarely painful, mine were horrendous, again I was told to go home and rest, I was even told to stop going to the hospital for every "little" pain. I wanted to scream that they weren't little! I consider myself to have a high pain threshold after dealing with 3 slipped discs which happened some years before, specialists couldn't believe I was capable of walking around due to the level of pain intensity from the damaged vertebrae, so I knew I wasn't imagining these pains. As soon as any medic found out this was my first pregnancy, they all gave me that same look that I was some kind of hypochondriac!

That night I was restless, I was uncomfortable and still in such extreme pain, I got up around 3am to go to the bathroom, as I stood up a gushing of warm water flowed out of me, my water broke! I awoke my partner, who for once wasn't drunk and we went to the hospital. Once in the maternity unit, I was told they had no beds, they tried phoning around to nearby hospitals, but the situation was the same. I was left in a corridor in a wheelchair and by this time I was having the most horrendous contractions and again feeling sick, I was curled up in a ball sitting down hugging my knees, this was the only position I could be in. I needed the bathroom and I was told I couldn't go, but I couldn't hold it in, and I didn't want to pee myself. I eventually managed to go to the toilet and once again I was bleeding but not only clots it was a lot of blood.

Nobody seemed to care as I sat in that corridor, nurses and doctors kept rushing past and I kept asking if it was my turn to be seen, but I just suddenly felt like a mute, nobody was listening and I could feel my baby pushing down, at the same time I was sitting in this chair covered in blood. I kept telling whoever would listen that I was bleeding, and I thought I was losing my baby, each and every time I was told I needed to wait and there was nothing they could do as they were so busy. I was sitting there crying my eyes out, I could sense my baby was dying, I had an immense gut feeling telling me this is not okay!

My partner was rarely around he kept going out to have a cigarette claiming *he* was nervous and stressed! I eventually got seen by a doctor that decided to give me an internal, at this point I was laying on a trolley, still in a corridor. I felt so undignified, people were walking around me and there I was laying in a busy corridor with not even a curtain around me. I was 3cm's dilated and was told that it was too early for me to give birth and that I should go home! I couldn't believe it, my water had broken, and I knew that the risk of infection afterwards is very high, I was also bleeding at this point quite heavily, but the doctor just got a nurse to give me a sanitary pad. They had no beds and they envisaged that I wasn't about to go full dilation anytime soon. I argued that I wasn't leaving, I was bleeding and in the most horrendous pain, I knew it wasn't just regular contraction pain. I became hysterical which is when a security guard had come over to my partner and told him we had to leave! For a moment I wished I was back in Lanzarote.

I refused to go home, I told my partner I would just wait in the car in the car park, that was my plan but as I got up my legs buckled, and I couldn't stand. I think it was a combination of stress, adrenaline and anxiety. A lovely midwife saw me and saw the state I was in, she said she would find me a bed and she did, it wasn't what I was expecting, it was literally a trolley put into a stock room with a curtain around, I didn't care at that point, I was just grateful for a bit of dignity. She also told me that the bleeding wasn't normal, and she would try to find a senior doctor, I felt so weak, my blood pressure was dropping, and I was feeling delirious and very faint.

I was hooked up to the monitor to keep an eye on the contractions, the nurses kept asking me for my birth plan, but I didn't have one, I still had 6 weeks to go, it was just one of those things I hadn't got around to doing, my sisters had epidurals and they told me they were amazing, so I guessed I would have one too. I asked the nurse for the injection, actually I didn't ask I think I begged her as I was in so much pain, she told me it was too early and instead gave me a pethidine injection. After about half an hour this intense pain just disappeared, I felt calm, I was still having contractions but they were now bearable, I think I must have dozed off but I was woken by intense pain again, the midwife checked me and said I wasn't dilated enough still and it would be a long time before my baby would show, I was crying in pain and I was exhausted, each and every nurse or midwife that I asked for help immediately asked me if it was my first pregnancy, as soon as I said yes their reply was the same, that the pain was normal. I'm sure they were thinking that I just had no clue and I was being annoying. I think I had about another 2 pethidine injections, which felt like they were only giving me to shut me up, every time I asked why I was bleeding, I was injected.

I needed more pain relief, I spotted the nice nurse and told her I didn't want more injections I just wanted to know if my baby was ok and then out came the gas and air. I was sucking on the pipe for dear life, it wasn't taking the pain away but for a split second it was giving me a lightheaded feeling which was making me forget the pain. The nurse kept yelling at me as I was constantly inhaling it, she said I was only allowed to have it with a contraction, but at this point I was too high off it to even care what she was saying.

Some time went by and the pain was back even stronger than ever, I felt like I needed to stand up and walk around, but every time I tried to I was told I had to lay down, laying down was the most uncomfortable position, I wanted to scream in pain but I didn't want to cause a scene, so I just cried as quietly as I could. My partner was useless, every word that came out of his mouth seemed to annoy the hell out of me, but I was so scared to be alone, so I just put up with him. A nurse came around and

I pleaded that I wanted the epidural, she kept telling me I had to wait, wait for what? I didn't understand and the staff were so rushed off their feet that nobody was explaining. Eventually after what felt like an eternity an anaesthetist turned up with the biggest needle I'd ever seen in my life, now I understood why I had to wait, he was obviously busy elsewhere.

I was told that I had to sit up straight and bend curled forward, I tried but it was too painful, the nurses were practically shouting at me, telling me if I wanted the injection I had to sit in this position, I was crying as each time I tried the pain ran straight through me, in the end they asked my partner to hold my arms pulled straight out in front of me while they helped me sit up. I was screaming out for them to stop and let me go, but they didn't, they just kept telling my partner to hold me tighter! I felt the needle going in, it felt like it was about 20 inches long, at the same time sitting up was giving me the most horrendous pain down below. It felt like pure torture, this wasn't how I expected labour to be, I didn't want to be manhandled, I was in pain, I was uncontrollably crying, and I knew my stress levels must be making my baby boy stressed too. The procedure was finally over and I was allowed to lay back down, instantly the pain had gone, it was a huge relief. The nurse decided to take a look down below, it was so weird I couldn't move my legs, I was completely paralysed. The look on the nurse's face was one of shock! The baby's head was down, so down in fact that's what was causing some of the extreme pain, I was actually sitting on my baby's head when I was in the curled-up position. Why didn't they check before they gave me the epidural, I could have crushed my baby's head with my weight!

The trolley I was laying on in the stock room, was suddenly wheeled into a treatment room. The baby heart monitor was hooked up around my bump, at this point I was still very drowsy and drugged up, so I wasn't aware of what was going on. All of a sudden what I can only describe as a crash team came barging into the room, there were 2 doctors in white coats, a midwife and several nurses. All I could see were faces looking down at me. I was so exhausted that my eyes felt very heavy and I was trying my hardest to focus. One doctor was explaining that my baby's heart had stopped and they needed to get him out, I wasn't dilated enough to push and she said she needed to cut me, I couldn't manage any words, it was a combination of being drugged up and being in shock. I remember my partner stood next to my head telling the doctor to just cut me, the next thing, I see a scalpel, I didn't feel the cut luckily thanks to the epidural. I felt my eyes rolling to the back of my head, I couldn't keep them still, all I could hear was the doctor telling me I needed to push, I couldn't even control my eyes open let alone control a push.

The moments that passed, felt like they were in slow motion, I could see people moving around me, checking my heart monitor, checking my drip, it felt like everybody was talking but I couldn't hear anything other than muffled sounds, my head felt floppy and all I can remember was the very bright lights in the ceiling. I remember looking at my partner and seeing the scared look on his face, I kept trying to speak to him, I wanted to ask what was going on, but I couldn't manage any sound, it was as though I had lost my voice.

I'm not quite sure how much time had gone past, but I remember the nurse giving me some kind of liquid in the cannula which was implanted in my hand, I suddenly could hear and everything came back to normal speed, the doctor began telling me they needed to force the delivery with a ventouse, I had no idea what this was at the time, but it's a suction device which they attach to the baby's head so they can pull him out. She was telling me I had to push once it was attached, I found it incredibly hard to push as I had no feeling down below, but I pushed as hard as I could. I was pushing so much I was shattered and then all of a sudden, I felt him being dragged out of me. I could see my tiny little blue baby put in what I can only describe as a big metal dish, being resuscitated, he wasn't crying he was quiet and motionless and doctors around him were pumping his tiny chest with their fingers. I was panicking I wanted to just get up and go to hold my baby, but I couldn't move. I was frantically looking at my partner urging him to do something, but he just stood there in shock. What felt like hours was probably only minutes and then all of a sudden, I heard a cry, my heart sank he was alive!

I just wanted to hold him, but they rushed him out of the room and into intensive care, I was told he was critical, and I had to be patient. Be patient, how could I be patient! Next I was told I had to deliver the placenta, I didn't even know I had to do this and I still couldn't feel down below, I had no energy to push so the midwife was frantically pressing down on my uterus with both of her hands, until it was all pulled out and placed on a dish. The midwife was examining the placenta and looked very concerned, she eventually explained that my placenta was broken and not intact as it should be, she was messing down below until she got it all out.

I had 13 stitches, luckily, I didn't feel a thing thanks to the epidural. The doctor came to see me and asked me to sign a form, I had no idea what I was signing but she said she would explain the next day, obviously when I wasn't so high off drugs. I didn't care for forms and stitches and placentas, all I wanted was my baby. He was on a ventilator and when they were happy enough with his breathing, I would then be able to hold him. Sometime had passed, hours I'm sure, I must've dozed off but I awoke to see that I was still on that same bed full of blood and my legs were still in stirrups, it was so incredibly degrading that I asked if I could at least have a sheet around me. I'm guessing I was there for so long afterwards as the hospital was so incredibly busy. I started getting feeling back down below, the epidural was wearing off.

Eventually, hours later my baby was brought to me, he was just perfect and able to breathe unaided. I held him in my arms and all the pain had literally seemed to wash away. I couldn't stop staring at him, he had a big red mark around his head from the ventouse and he looked slightly jaundiced, but apart from that I was filled with the most overwhelming love. He was only 2.2 kg and I was told that if I didn't breastfeed him, he would need to go back into intensive care to be fed through a tube. There was no way I was having him taken away from me again and I had already decided to breastfeed. As soon as I tried, he latched on and it just felt the most natural thing in the world.

I was finally cleaned up and moved to a ward, I had to keep waking him every few hours to feed, all he wanted to do was sleep. He was just perfect in every way, as soon as I saw his face, I decided he was a Tyler. My partner went home as it was very late, I was in labour for a total of 19 hours, I didn't expect him to be 6 weeks premature and all the clothes I had bought were way too big, the plan was he was to go shopping the next morning for prem clothes and come back first thing.

The next morning the doctor came to see me, she explained that during my pregnancy the placenta hadn't developed as it should have and placental abruption had occurred, this all meant nothing to me but she continued to explain that the placenta was separating from the inner wall of my uterus, which was blocking the baby's supply of oxygen and nutrients, this was also the reason for the heavy bleeding and the excruciating pain. She said it was a miracle that he survived, and she wanted to explain why she needed to use assistance with the ventouse to deliver him. He had died and she also informed me that my own heart rate was slowing down too, so when my eyes were rolling to the back of my head, that wasn't the effect of the drugs, that was my heart stopping. We were both extremely lucky, we could've both died before childbirth. The doctor also praised me for being able to push when I did in the state that I was in myself. If I hadn't the end result could have been different. Somebody up there was definitely looking over me and guided me along the way. Placental abruption is very rare, happening with only 1% of pregnancies. I did actually look into this weeks later and the symptoms were all what I was experiencing, the pain, the bleeding, the early contractions. Instead of any doctors taking me seriously, I was shunned because it was my first pregnancy and I was made to feel stupid and a timewaster.

I had a few family visitors come to see us, my partner however was nowhere in sight, in fact he didn't come to see us until 2 days after I'd given birth, he went out to celebrate and even when he did eventually turn up, he was stinking of booze and I didn't want him anywhere near us! After about 4 days in the hospital we were discharged, at the hospital Tyler literally did nothing but sleep, I thought I was so lucky to have such a good baby, when all the other babies on the ward seemed to be crying a lot especially for feeds, I was having to wake Tyler up for his feed, I knew if I didn't as he was premature they would keep him in, so I was determined to make sure he was fed enough. Whilst I was in hospital, with Tyler sleeping most of the time, I actually slept fairly well as I was hooked up to painkillers the whole time, so I didn't notice the rawness I had down below. Plus, I wasn't doing anything strenuous, just laying next to my quiet baby.

After a few days of being home, Tyler soon discovered a voice! And he cried a lot...

It took me a good few weeks to realise that whilst I thought Tyler was such a golden baby the first days of his life not crying, the real reason was because he was heavily sedated from the drugs I was given during labour, all the pethidine, gas and air and epidural given to me was obviously passed down into his own bloodstream, if you can imagine the effect they had on me, I'm not surprised why he was pretty much comatose for those first days with him being so tiny and taking the high amount of these drugs. I also didn't realise the extent of how traumatic the whole pregnancy and birth was. Of course, it didn't help that I was in such a bad relationship and I was constantly stressed.

The first couple of weeks after the birth were horrendous, I had dissolvable stitches which they said would soon disintegrate, but in the meantime it was so incredibly sore and painful, the worst was when I was I trying to sit up to breastfeed, any pressure from sitting was just hell, I was scared to pee because it stung so badly, I was also anaemic, a problem that I suffered for years before I was pregnant, I lost so much blood during childbirth that they really should've given me a blood transfusion, but instead they opted to give me iron tablets, which didn't agree with me and made me constipated which didn't help the issues down below. I felt rough, weak and very tired. Tyler was waking practically every 2 hours for feeds, I hardly had any help at home, family came to visit and even offered for me to sleep for a few hours during the day whilst they kept an eye on Tyler, but for some reason I refused, I thought I would feel like a failure if I accepted help, looking back now I should've received all the help offered. My partner was still being an absolute dick and wasn't helping around the house at all, he was actually barely home, and I was struggling to cope looking after a newborn baby and caring for myself.

I knew things had to change at home and once again fuelled by hormones and not thinking straight, I gave my partner an ultimatum if he wanted to be in mine and our sons lives, he had to stop drinking! I wished I was strong enough to just tell him to leave, but I was frightened to be alone. However, he did actually stop drinking and whilst he never did much around the house or with Tyler, just having him there made me feel that I was completely alone.

After Tyler was born, I kept reliving the horrific labour and birth experience, so much so that it was difficult to sleep, I rarely slept anyway as Tyler was waking throughout the night. Sometimes I would dream of taking a sleeping pill so I could have a good night's sleep, the lack of sleep made me anxious and stressed, I wouldn't allow my partner to feed Tyler during the night, I didn't want him out of my sight for a minute, I felt that because I couldn't control the pregnancy or birth, I needed to be able to control his care.

I knew I was suffering from post-traumatic stress disorder, I remember going to my doctor who prescribed me anti-depressants, which I didn't take I knew I would become hooked on them and I didn't want to be dependent on a drug, instead I just quietly dealt with the war I was having in my mind, I kept going over and over the finer details, did I do something wrong? did I cause these placenta issues? was it all the stress I was in? I had all these questions which remained unanswered, which I went over and over again. I felt like I had failed my pregnancy so I was determined that I wasn't going to fail motherhood; I secretly cried, that was my release, it became a habit, I could only sleep if I cried myself to sleep. Everybody kept telling me these emotions were normal and that they would pass, but I never told anyone how deep down I was really feeling, I just agreed that I was tired, it was easier than explaining.

During my pregnancy, because I wasn't maternal, I dreaded the fact that I may reject my baby – as I had read does happen, but I think because of how difficult my pregnancy and birth was, I took to motherhood like a duck to water, despite the tiredness and uncomfortability of the afterbirth. I loved being a mom and I felt an overwhelming urge to protect him as much as I could. When Tyler was 4 months old, I decided to move back abroad, because I was feeling so depressed and still reliving the awful birth, in my head I thought if I was in a different environment all those bad memories would fade away.

We went back to Tenerife. I was to return to work and his dad would look after him during the day. This worked out for only a few months and before I knew it, he was back to his usual selfish drunken self. I wasn't happy at all, but I just put up with things and I still couldn't get my head straight.

The next 2 years were hell, we kept breaking up and getting back together, I knew it was detrimental to not only my health but for Tyler's early foundation years. I made a decision that he had to leave once and for all and he did, it was just me and Tyler and it felt so much better. Two weeks after we separated, I felt faint and tired, I knew that feeling… I was pregnant.

After a lot of deliberating, I had decided to go ahead with the pregnancy, I knew deep down that I would never have another child and I didn't want Tyler to be an only child, so I decided to have this baby for him so he could grow up with a sibling. After my bad experience with the first pregnancy I was determined that this time around would be textbook perfect. I had private medical insurance at that point, so I could use a private hospital, I knew the standard of care would be better and I knew that the staff in private hospitals also spoke English.

This pregnancy was so much different, I was single, but I was stress free. I had a childminder look after Tyler and his dad rarely bothered to see him. It suited me just fine, the less I saw of him, the less stress I would feel. This time around was such a contrast to the last, I made sure I ate healthily, and I swam every day. I also had a check-up every month, each hospital visit would still dread me with fear, and I made sure that they checked that the placenta was always intact. I was having a girl, I felt incredibly lucky to be having a sister for Tyler.

A month before my due date, I needed to weigh up my birth plan options, after Tyler's disastrous birth, I wanted the second time around to be completely opposite, so I decided to have a natural birth. I read up on ways to breath when the contractions started, to be able to control the pain, why this was never mentioned to me when I was going through labour with Tyler I'll never know. Breathing is the most natural way to control most things going on within, stress, anxiety, pain...

I started contractions at home 2 weeks early, I didn't rush to the hospital like I did before, I waited until they were very close. In hospital, I explained that no matter how much I called out in pain, they were to not give me any medication at all. The nurses agreed but did advise that if I wanted an epidural one would be on standby. There was no way I was having that again!

After Tyler's birth, I had incredible back pain, my degenerative disc disease from the slipped vertebrae was affected by the injection, a chiropractor had explained that an epidural should never be given to people with slipped discs as it could cause permanent paralysis. Again, I was so lucky!

As I was in a private hospital, I had my own room, the midwife wasn't patronising at all like they were in the UK hospital, I was allowed to give birth at my own pace and in my own way. I just kept saying I wanted it to be as relaxed as possible. I had dimmed lights, candles and very soft music, I was allowed to walk around and get in any position that I wanted. The midwife told me she would only intervene if I needed her to, it felt so right.

I was walking around the room and allowing gravity to do its job, I'm not going to lie, it wasn't the most comfortable at times, but I concentrated on my breathing. When I felt the urge to push, I called the nurse who checked and just like that I was 10cm's dilated. I had the choice to give birth laying down or standing up crouched over the bed, I chose to lay down. After a couple of pushes she was born, my beautiful baby girl, my beautiful Layla. I didn't even need any stitches; this was how labour and birth was supposed to be.

My second pregnancy whilst was a breeze in comparison to my first, was still doused with the rawness of Tyler's birth. The closer I got to my due date, the more I felt myself becoming frightened of the what if's that were about to happen. My decision for a natural birth was mainly because I didn't want my unborn baby to be flooded with medication, but it was also because I wanted to be clear headed and on the ball, not drugged up like I was with Tyler.

As soon as Layla was born all those bad memories and visions had faded away and into the back of my distant memory and I've not thought about that traumatic birth which haunted me for years up until writing this chapter now.

I now have closure.

★★★

Dee Mani-Mitchell is a mom, health advocate and author. In 2017, Dee developed Triple Negative breast cancer, deemed the most aggressive cancer type. After refusing a cocktail of conventional medicine, (chemotherapy and radiotherapy), Dee healed herself within 5 months, completely naturally using a range of alternative medicine.

Since then, as a published author, Dee aims to create a better understanding of our health, our world and our place in it – a mission which has cast Dee in many different roles: author, motivator, inspirer and awareness raiser.

Dee can be contacted via her website at www.deemani.com

Elaine

Two Birth Traumas and an OBE

I never really thought about my experiences as being 'birth trauma' until this term was raised by Jessica. In fact, I've had two of them!

My daughter was born in May 1982 and I endured such a dreadful time, I vowed I would never go through that malarkey again. However, 12 years later, my son arrived in September 1994. The difference this time, was that I was in control, knew what was likely to happen and I wasn't scared or misinformed.

No-one could say that I am a maternal person by any stretch of the imagination. I am not particularly fond of pets either. People are OK but babies bore me until they start being interesting by doing and saying things that are cute or cheeky. If I have to interact with children, I can cope with them in a school setting around the ages of 11 to 12 or 15-16 when they are becoming curious about life and are willing and interested to learn from old fossils like me, how to get on in the world.

When my daughter was born, I was in the fortunate position of being a successful business owner and employed a Nanny to look after her so that I could carry on running my enterprise. When my son was born, his Father was (still is) a fantastic musician and a stay at home Dad, while I was employed running a huge team for an organisation in London. One Saturday, my son pushed me away because he didn't want me around – he didn't know me and saw me as an intruder in our home. I left for work before he awoke and often arrived home after he'd gone to bed. No wonder he didn't recognise me! We didn't know at the time that he had a medical condition, we just thought we had a challenging and spirited child.

It could be said that I should never have had children, or even got married. My first husband recently acknowledged that I'm a free spirit who is not designed to be tied down. So how did I end up with two beautiful children, and why were their births traumatic?

In my teens, my Mother encouraged me to go to the family planning clinic when I had set my first wedding date. My Dad become incapacitated with cancer between my engagement date and sadly died six months before the wedding. I was very careful to take the contraceptive pill because I knew that I wasn't going to be married for long and didn't want to be saddled with a child and feel honour bound to stay in a marriage that wasn't going to last.

As I walked down the aisle in 1976, I was crying my eyes out. I could hear people in the church pews saying, 'oh she's missing her Dad'. Yes of course I was, but I was also crying because I knew I would be hurting so many people, especially the man I was about to marry. We'd been together for five years. We were school sweethearts and did the expected thing in those days; saved up at the local building society, put our names down on the waiting list for a mortgage, announced our engagement and then planned our wedding. Dad had a cancer diagnosis and my first husband was amazing in helping us to look after Dad at home when the cancer spread to his brain. He'd already had his leg amputated by this stage and so getting to the bathroom and attending to other personal needs on one leg was a challenge. As you can imagine, life at home was difficult and although Dad's cancer spread to his brain and he was hallucinating, he made it quite clear to me, before his brain deterioration that my fiancée was not the right man for me. Despite this, Dad gave us both his blessing. At least I had the sense to maintain what I'd learned at the family planning clinic to save further upset after our marriage. I am not proud of my actions. My only defence is that I was exceedingly vulnerable and under great pressure from family to continue with the wedding six months after Dad's passing. Steve and I remain friends to this day, and when my Mum died suddenly in 2015, he was one of the pallbearers and he and his wife made the flowers for the coffin which was a replica of Mum's wedding bouquet to my Dad.

Business

After walking away from my first marriage and being single again for a short while, I met my second husband at work. We decided to leave and start our own business which became successful quite quickly. We married in 1980 on the very same day that Steve remarried.

Charlotte's Father, my second husband, was 9 years older than me and not keen to have children. His Mother was surprised and delighted in equal measure when we announced I was expecting. I assumed that one day I would become a Mother but never planned when this would be.

The business grew swiftly. I don't recall the precise position of the business at the time I became pregnant but suffice to say that we had a few staff and I had a personal assistant which was very handy. Louise used to visit me in hospital where I remained for 10 weeks during my confinement. Her visits enabled me to carry on running the business from my private hospital room. The internet wasn't available to the public at this stage, and mobile phones were the size of bricks. We relied on landlines, letters or in-person to communicate, so you can appreciate how important her visits were to me, and the business.

The business had a variety of different aspects to it. We grew to own four kitchen showrooms, a manufacturing plant and a construction division that supplied and fitted kitchens into new buildings or refurbishments. There were no business mentors in those days and accountants only looked backwards. We had no business support or previous business experience of any description, yet somehow, we managed to thrive until 1986 when things went wrong, but that's another story.

Swimming and Kidneys

When I was around nine years old, I was selected by the swimming club coach as 'one to watch'. My breaststroke was considered the perfect style, although the accepted style today is more like butterfly and completely different at competition level.

I trained twice daily, represented my County at National level and often had urinary infections and projectile vomiting which was put down to the chlorine and other chemicals in the water, as well as a condition called Salpingitis. A spinster medical specialist, Miss Margaret Witt from North Middlesex hospital, diagnosed Salpingitis in my early teens. She claimed that the only way I could have contracted this condition which affects the fallopian tubes is by sleeping around. How dare she?! I was a good girl – honestly – no, really, I was! I googled Salpingitis to find this common description…

> *Salpingitis* is inflammation of the fallopian tubes, caused by bacterial infection. Common causes of *salpingitis* include sexually transmitted diseases such as gonorrhoea and chlamydia.

My distrust of the medical profession continues to this day.

Around the age of 21 I was feeling ill more often and one day things became so bad I dialled 999 and was taken by ambulance with the blue light flashing to St Anne's hospital in Tottenham, North London. I was placed in an isolation ward because it was thought I may have an infectious disease called Typhoid. After many tests it transpired that the cause of my problem for many years was a condition called Medullary Sponge Kidneys. Dr Google again…

> *Medullary sponge kidney* is a congenital *disorder* of the *kidneys* characterized by cystic dilatation of the collecting tubules in one or both *kidneys.* Individuals with *medullary sponge kidney* are at increased risk for *kidney* stones and urinary tract infection (UTI).

The only person I've ever met who knew about the condition was the nurse who checked me in for my mastectomy years later, and she'd had a kidney removed. So, the years of discomfort and embarrassment turned out to be a condition that I was born with, hallelujah, I now knew what I was dealing with, but what has this all to do with birth trauma you may well ask?

Remember me saying that I was in confinement for 10 weeks? Well that was because of my kidneys.

Rewind to my correct diagnosis; I was referred to a Consultant Urologist who looked after me for many years until he retired and passed me to another consultant specialist. I was put on antibiotics and told I'd be on them for the rest of my life because my kidney condition was incurable. I'd see the consultant every six months and every now and then I had a special type of x-ray in which dye was injected to clearly show up how my kidneys were functioning. Both specialists maintained the same view of my condition, although I was allergic to the dye which uses iodine and so the x-rays stopped. The only other way to have this test was to have injections that cost £000s because the dye included a substance made from gold which was not considered cost effective.

Charlotte

When I became pregnant, the kidney specialist suggested that a different type of antibiotic would be better for the health of my baby. It took a great deal of trial and error to find the right drug for me. I don't recall the details but eventually, I was taken into hospital at around 29 weeks into the pregnancy because of concern for me and the baby. It seemed like every day I was tested for something or other.

My private room made things more bearable and I was able to have visitors whenever I wanted. This was helpful from a business perspective as Louise, my PA, came in every day at different times. My Mum and her then husband (a mistake on the rebound after my Dad died) were visiting down from the guest house they ran in Keswick in The Lake District.

My due date came and went and eventually in the early hours of Thursday morning 20th May 1982 the birth was induced by what seemed to be a crochet hook – ouch! There was no pre discussion about my wishes and no specific midwife had been assigned to me. Throughout the day medical staff spoke around me, not to me. I became worried for both of us, until I was finally taken into a delivery room, and then I became even more concerned!

Again, a series of medical people came and went in and out of the small room. It seemed very crowded. At one time, Mum and Jim came in to deliver a gift; as ever the practical person, Mum had brought in a collection of nappies, baby creams and powders and a few baby clothes. She was also concerned because they had guests to prepare for and unless I performed that day, they would be returning to Keswick without seeing their grandchild or knowing if everything was alright.

My pain was getting worse, yet there was no sign of movement. It was decided that I would have an epidural injection. To this day I have a numb area on my back caused by the procedure. The labour continued with little movement to the point where the epidural wore off. A specialist Obstetrician was called in and husband of the day was evicted because he became abusive to the staff. He never wanted to be present at the delivery and was there under sufferance in the first place. The owner of a dry cleaner shop in Chingford once threatened to call the police on him because of his ranting that they couldn't clean his special coat in time. I was glad for him to leave and let me get on with what I had to do as I had no doubt the police may have be needed again by the way he was carrying on.

You can imagine my level of stress by this stage in the proceedings.

My baby girl was finally delivered at six minutes to midnight and weighed 6lb 12oz. Remarkably she was fine, but I was not.

The problem transpired to be her short umbilical cord and her position. Instead of facing up, her position was face down. The medics were unable to move her but didn't know why. To manually adjust her, they cut me from front to back (22 stiches were needed). During this time, I found myself looking down on the whole debacle from a position to the right of me up on the ceiling to where I had floated. I since learned that this was an OBE (out of body experience) and can happen when you have a near death experience. My daughter was taken away, checked over and cleaned while the consultant undertook manual removal of the placenta – more ouch!

I recall being left covered in blood and completely on

my own in the delivery room at one point. The rest is blank. Charlotte is now 37 and has blossomed into a beautiful soul, despite my poor maternal instincts.

Andrew

I vowed never to have any more children. The dramatic events of Charlotte's birth had scarred me. However, my third husband was such a gentle man and a stark contrast to Charlotte's Father – remember the man who I ran the business with who was evicted from the delivery room because of his abusive behaviour?!

We were having an extension built at home so that my husband's elderly aunt could come and live with us. The builder kept talking so proudly about his son and I could sense that my husband was interested. He was a great stepfather to Charlotte. In fact, Charlotte came home from school one day and had changed her name to his on her schoolbooks without any discussion. My husband and I discussed having a child and I became pregnant with our son.

The pregnancy went OK as far as I recall. I had the same kidney drug challenges but by this time the medical profession had moved on and they knew what to do with my situation. I was running a busy department at a law firm in London and carried on working until the day before the planned caesarean section on September 6th, 1994. Again, I was in a fortunate position. My employer sent the firm's chauffeur to collect me some mornings in the beautiful air-conditioned Jaguar after I'd had a panic attack on the tube.

I've always had problems with my spine. I have a mild form of spina bifida at the base, lordosis and scoliosis (and recently a fractured spine). In the distant past I have been hospitalised and put on traction and drugs to manage my pain and immobilisation. Today I manage by fortnightly visits to a chiropractor and regular use of my Powertube – a device which relieves pain and changes the underlying molecules to optimise my wellbeing. I went ahead with the pregnancy on the basis that I wasn't going to go through the same horror of when Charlotte was delivered. My spine condition had worsened and so a natural birth would have put more strain on it. Discussions were held with my specialist team and reluctantly they agreed, at my insistence, to a planned caesarean section.

Husband of the day was with me in the delivery room, and all appeared to go well. I had an epidural procedure which meant that I could be awake. Mum appeared in the after-delivery suite and called the nurses over to comment that Andrew was purple – why had I not seen this? Andrew was taken away quickly to the NICU special care ward (neonatal intensive care unit) where he remained for 9 days because of low oxygen readings. My back had not fared well after all and I couldn't walk. I was given a Polaroid photo of my new baby and sent to a shared ward where other Mothers had their babies with them. All I had was my photograph. I didn't even have many visitors because some of them just went straight to the NICU ward, including my husband. It was a miserable time and I still feel sad when I think about it. I only remember seeing Andrew once when a wheelchair became available and my husband pushed me delicately over every lump and bump through the hospital to the NICU ward.

We both recovered and within 10 days I was working from home. The IT department had set up a home computer for me so that I could continue working. I was not cut out for baby talk. I needed more stimulation in a grown-up world. By this time, we had desktop computers and email, although it was not terribly good over the dial up internet that was still in its infancy. Andrew's Father gave up work to concentrate on his music within a short time of us meeting and thus became a stay-at-home Dad which suited us all.

It took many years to understand his behaviour but at the age of 12 Andrew was diagnosed with a form of autism called Asperger's Syndrome.

Afterward

I am now 62 and have decided not to have any more children! I remain friends with all three of my ex-husbands. Andrew has a challenging life which saddens me daily. Charlotte is mother to two delightful teenage boys but lost her 17-month-old daughter following her MMR jab in 2010.

I remain happily single and now focus on building an online natural health hub. I provide support and mentoring to individuals and families struggling with health challenges or to those who want to avoid them in the first place. Using my skills and experience as a Business Psychologist and Nutritionist, I have reinvented myself as a Master Wellness Mentor following recovery from four bouts of cancer and curing my kidney condition naturally over 20 years ago. My online Wellness HUB and CLUB enable individuals to achieve and maintain Perfect Health from home 24/7.

***

Elaine Godley is a Master Wellness Mentor, radio show host and Amazon #1 best-selling author, who has beaten cancer four times, and cured herself of a serious kidney disease. A qualified Nutritionist, Psychologist, former Athlete and Business Consultant, Elaine has an all-round appreciation of

how to achieve and maintain your own Perfect Health. Elaine mentors individuals on how to recover from cancer or avoid it in the first place via her online health hub.
www.perfect-health.co.uk

Aime

I'm a planner at heart, you know, the boring sensible one. I worked hard at school, went to Uni, got a job, bought a house, got married. Next on the list was kids. My darling husband (DH) and I had always wanted kids, I think we talked about it on about our second date! I am one of three and couldn't imagine life without children. We are a great team, DH and me. I'm the optimist, he is more of a pessimist, so he had already worked out that if it took longer than two years to try for a baby, that was when we could go to the Dr's and ask for IVF, he'd had mumps as a kid and was certain that we would struggle. So, we started trying as soon as we were married, not that we particularly felt we needed to be married, it was more of a practical issue of knowing weddings were big things to organise! Six weeks after I came off the pill, I was pregnant, we were both quite shocked. I kind of felt guilty that it had happened so quickly, and I usually don't tell people. I know how hard it is for some people to get pregnant, and I've been so lucky in life, it didn't feel fair that we got pregnant so easily as well. DH walked round on cloud nine for about a week, he was so pleased and relieved that it was all going to work out. We didn't know anyone who had kids, we were the first of our friends to get pregnant, we were both 27 when Emily was born. We didn't know about the miscarriage statistics, or that we should wait to tell people until 12-weeks, so we told family and friends.

I found pregnancy exhausting. I have never been slim, and

I was a lot bigger than I wanted to be when I got pregnant, I also had a big job in Local Government. I had only been in the job a few weeks when I had to tell my new boss I was pregnant because I felt so sick and exhausted and I thought I'd better tell her what was going on. Considering I'd only just started she took it pretty well. I ate far too much during my pregnancy and was tired ALL the time. I remember going to bed as soon as I got home from work, waking up for about an hour for dinner, then sleeping through till I had to get up from work the next day. Other than that, I had a relatively stress-free pregnancy.

About three weeks before Emily was due, I went in for a final midwife check-up. They were training a new midwife and she kept struggling to catch Emily's heartbeat, we heard it loud and strong, but not for long enough. After what seemed like about half an hour the midwife explained it was protocol that I should go to the hospital for a scan, she didn't think there was anything to worry about, but she just wanted to play it safe. I drove myself to the hospital and asked DH to meet me there. They saw me very quickly and I was in and out in a flash, but they asked me to see the Dr, I was a bit worried, but not too much as I had heard Emily's heart beating loudly as they scanned me. Scans aren't typically done this late in a pregnancy, and they estimated that three weeks before my due date she was already between 10 and 12 lbs.

What! I'm 5ft 4, and although well covered, of slight build, how the hell was a 12 lb baby going to come out of me? I wasn't expecting the delivery to be pain free, but surely the level of pain might well correlate with the size of the baby? By the time DH got to the hospital I was already starting to worry about what problems such a large baby could cause. I'd been cleared of gestational diabetes, but I couldn't help wondering if my weight was somehow a factor. Later I found out my Gran had been 11 lbs even though my Great Gran was shorter than me and she was born during the first world war, so it was probably more of a genetic thing, but… The Dr's weren't very helpful, but I did the awful thing of looking up big babies on the internet, and quickly learnt that I was far more likely to have problems delivering. Great!

Monday 17th May 2004, I woke early and thought I'd wet myself. But no, my waters had broken. We rang the hospital and they said I had to come in just to check me over, but that they would probably discharge me afterwards. When I got to the hospital, they said I hadn't started to dilate at all and went to get the discharge papers. By the time they came back, I'd had two massive contractions and dilated to 4cms. I wasn't going anywhere. At this point I handed over my birth plan (how amusingly naive) and said I'd like a water birth. From this point on things didn't really go to plan. I learnt afterwards that it isn't advised to go into a birth pool until you are at least 5cms dilated as it can slow the delivery down too much, and that is exactly what happened. I was also supposed to be supervised, but the hospital was short-staffed the night Emily was born, and I just had a series of midwives pop in to check on me. About six hours later, my labour having not progressed at all, I was told I had to get out of the pool. After about another twelve hours they started getting worried and said that they needed to speed things along. I basically felt that they just needed the bed. I'm not sure what drug they gave me but suddenly everything started happening fast and I was in agony. I couldn't cope with this, and was already exhausted, so asked for some pain relief. They decided to give me an epidural, which they did. When the anaesthetist came back, I said that it hadn't worked. Patronisingly he told me that there may still be some pain. I nearly bit his head off (pregnant lady in labour, you'd have thought he would have known better). I told him I wasn't an idiot and that the pain level hadn't changed at all, not one little bit. As he absorbed this, he went very pale and ran out of the room. I found out later that an epidural gone wrong could have paralysed me if he'd put it in the wrong place, which is what he thought he might have done if it hadn't worked. There was then an emergency meeting outside my room, and he came back in to tell me that I could have another one, which I did. Fortunately, this one worked, but it worked too well. I wasn't in pain, but I was totally numb from my waist down. I had no idea when my contractions were and had no urge to push. Again, I should have had a midwife with me constantly at this point, but again they were short-staffed.

Not knowing when to push, and abandoned, nothing much happened, but Emily started getting into distress. Yes, I was 10cms dilated, but I hadn't dilated fully (there was a lip), and they suspected at this point that I might not dilate fully, so they decided to take me to the operating theatre to try a forceps delivery, but in the theatre so they could quickly move onto a C-section if they needed to. By this point they had attached a heart monitor to Emily's head by essentially hooking it into the skin on her skull (which I wasn't impressed by when I found out later). They tried the forceps, and a ventouse, but it didn't work, well not totally, they kind of got her half out then decided that they would push her back in and do a C-section anyway.

I had the common sense not to look at my reflection in the lights as Emily was delivered. It felt like they were washing up in my belly, but I was exhausted, and I just wanted to see my daughter and get out of there. Eventually there she was, my beautiful, healthy, amazing daughter, all 9lb 7 oz of her.

I hadn't planned to have a C-section, I hadn't read up on it, and my NCT classes, so against C-sections, hadn't discussed it at all. I knew that Emily was ok, but that I had lost a lot of blood (they almost did a transfusion) but that was it. Nobody told me what a C-section meant. After the haze of family visits a very stressed and exhausted DH went home for some sleep and I found myself alone with Emily on the ward in the middle of the night. I had a catheter and was hooked up to pain relief via an IV. For some strange reason they had put Emily at the foot of my bed. She woke crying, I didn't know if it was safe for me to get out of bed, so I pressed the call button and asked. An angry nurse, clearly irritated to be summoned told me in no uncertain terms that I was quite capable of looking after my daughter on my own and flounced off. I burst into tears, the emotions, the pain, the fear, the utter sense of being alone descended on me all at once. The reality that I'd nearly died, and could have been paralysed, that Emily had been distressed and DH had found watching the whole process deeply traumatising just collapsed on me all at once. But I was a Mum, and I loved my daughter, so I dragged myself out of bed, accidently disconnecting the catheter and dragging the IV, I staggered to the end of the bed, and tried to drag the crib next to me. Giving up, I leant in, picked Emily up, walked carefully back, and unable to get myself back in bed carrying Emily, collapsed into the chair. I sat there and held her for the rest of the night.

The next few days passed in a blur. The hospital was an awful place to be, noisy, yet lonely, Emily and I had to stay in for five days because she was jaundiced. I struggled to breastfeed, and the food was terrible (white spam sandwich anyone?). I just wanted to get home. Eventually they discharged us at midnight. A strange time to be discharged, still high on the drugs I hallucinated, but we were home. The next few days were lovely. I healed quickly, DH was happy and attentive, and Emily was an absolute delight.

Like many new mums, I didn't want to think about the experience of giving birth, I'd survived it, Emily had survived it, it was over. In relation to some people's stories, I suspect mine isn't so terrible. I wasn't left with any lasting trauma or PSTD but now many years on I look back and think it really didn't need to be as difficult as it was. After Emily was born, I worked in the NHS in management for almost four years, and I realised that although the NHS is fabulous at giving medical care, it often isn't great at supporting people holistically. It is an unwieldy system made up of many amazing and caring people, but too often patients are treated as products in a manufacturing line, done to, not with. Had there been more staff on that night, and more care been taken with protocols I wouldn't have gone into the birthing pool, and my labour may have proceeded naturally. I was lucky that the epidural gone wrong caused no harm, but I could have been paralysed, and with the cervix issue, trying to drag Emily out with both a ventouse and forceps could have caused her harm. There was no need to put Emily at the foot of my bed, someone should have explained what the implications of an emergency C-section were and there was simply no need to shame me for not getting out of bed. Being a mum is tough enough without such unkindness. I never did manage to breastfeed (although I expressed for weeks, so I know she did get some of the good stuff) but maybe I would have been able to had things not been so difficult, or if we could have gone home more quickly.

When I got pregnant for a second time we were over the moon. We'd moved to Leicester by then and I was determined that it wouldn't be so bad second time round. I researched C-sections and found that the statistical chances of me having another were very high, and that most of the risks were to me, not the baby. Yes there is some evidence that the squeeze of the birth canal might help with lungs, and that all that blood and gunk helps seed the microbiome, but I was pretty sure that I could help get any kid dirty enough to have a healthy immune system, and there were far more risks to me and the baby if my cervix didn't dilate properly again and I had another baby. I wanted to manage my risks, the worst possible outcome for me was another awful labour AND another C-section. I'd made my mind up I wanted a C-section. The Dr had other ideas, no doubt spurred on by targets and the paternalistic bullshit around women delivering the natural way with pain being good for everyone (yes, let's go back to the natural way, premodern medicine when 10% of women died in childbirth). What didn't help was that they couldn't find my notes. Apparently, they didn't manage to transfer them, despite having 9 months to do so. They asked DH and me for details of all the drugs I was given, seriously, did they really expect us to remember all that? That is the whole point of having medical notes. I wasn't impressed that they'd lost them. I wanted a C-section, the Dr told me I wouldn't bond with my child if I had a C-section. Again, yes I know there is some evidence that this can be a problem, but maybe that was just the trauma, and quite frankly I found it insulting that some man was telling me what I should do with my body because I wouldn't be a good enough mother if I did it my way. Sod him, I would love this kid just as much as I did the last one, with every ounce of my being. If men had babies, they'd have discovered a way to do a C-section that was completely safe and pain free by now! By this time I was a senior manager in the NHS, I knew my arguments and I knew that if I got high enough in the management chain they would cave, scared that if they forced me to give birth naturally and it went wrong I'd sue. Jazzy was due on 26th December, planned C-sections (especially if there is potentially an issue around a large baby) are usually scheduled in a couple of weeks early. They scheduled me in for 24th December, I'm convinced they thought I was just trying to have a baby early to miss Christmas and thought they could "punish me" by booking it so late, that I might just go into labour anyway.

We arranged with Santa to come to our house early that year. On 23rd December Santa came for a very excited 3-year-old Emily, we had Christmas dinner and watched a bond film. On 24th December I went into hospital. It was a totally different experience, there was Christmas music playing in the operating theatre, a lovely anaesthetist called Amy and a festive and relaxed atmosphere. All went well, and Jazzy Lila Eve was born on Christmas Eve. Within 48 hours I was at home, almost pain free.

You may have sensed that there is some anger, a sense of indignation at the inherent sexism of the medical system and you'd be right. Too often women's heart attacks are misdiagnosed as being emotional issues, and almost 10 times as much medical research has been done on erectile dysfunction when compared with PMS or the menopause. Medical research and drug testing is almost always done on men despite the fact drugs often react differently in women's bodies. I am not the most natural of mums, I was never going to be the kind of woman who was mostly at home knee deep in nappies and messy play, but then why should I be? Why is there just one way to be a good mum? I love them both deeply and fiercely, I've taught them maths and impendence as well as how to make a gingerbread house. Birth by its very nature can be a risky business but let's find a way to do it with care, and love, supporting women and their partners, providing the best medical attention, but also ensuring that the experience is no more traumatic than it has to be. Emily's birth was unnecessarily traumatic, and I know some women have had much worse, but I fear that plenty more will have experienced a mildly traumatic birth like I did, and frankly I think we can, we should, we must do better.

★★★

Aime Armstrong is a Mum of two fabulous daughters. Based in the UK, Aime is on a mission to reduce conflict at work by encouraging healthy and supportive workplace relationships through training and people centred HR.

Emma

It was my first child and I really didn't have a clue what to expect from pregnancy or from the birth itself.

I had a picture in my mind that it would be a beautiful experience, I would be glowing and happy throughout my pregnancy, I would have a natural birth without complications and would instantly take to motherhood with my happy beautiful baby that would sleep all the time.

I mean that's the impression you get from watching movies, and photos you see of women pre and post birth, glowing and happy. But the reality of it was very different.

I had never been the one to gush over new babies or get broody when everyone around me was having children.

I didn't even like children that much if I'm honest, apart from the ones that were in my close family or friendship circle.

I just didn't understand how to relate to babies or children, but when I found out I was pregnant my stomach filled with excited butterflies and I looked forward to the joy, happiness, wonderful memories and challenges my baby would bring.

The reality though for me was very different.

Problems with my pregnancy started from just 6 weeks, I started to get severe back pain and found out I had pelvic girdle pain and sciatica, and as you may know, you are pretty limited to the painkillers you can take throughout pregnancy.

The pain gradually became worse throughout the pregnancy

and when I was only five months pregnant I couldn't walk far at all without crutches to get around.

Pain became part of my everyday life, it took over my body, consumed me and took over my whole body and my thoughts.

I couldn't wait to get my baby out, I started to resent the baby that was inside me and this led me into a dark deep pit of despair and misery. I became a shell of who I was before, and the guilt was taking over me. I was supposed to love my baby, the life that was growing inside of me, I was supposed to feel joy but instead all I felt was hate for my baby and for myself.

I have always struggled with my mental health even from a young age. I can remember when I was a teenager in high school, and I was getting bullied. I was different from everyone else; I didn't fit in, I was a nerd, quiet, reserved, had different opinions and preferred spending my time reading books.

I was so desperate to fit in, but I never did, I spent my time looking in from the outside wondering when I would ever feel whole, when was my time to be a part of something. Lonely and feeling like no one in the world understood me, I thought it was all my fault.

From such a young age I felt like I must have done something to deserve all the hate, longing for someone to connect with but not understanding how to connect.

One day I sat on my bed with tears streaming down my face, I hated myself, I hated the reflection looking back at me, I understood why no one liked me and why I was alone.

I just wanted it to stop so I sat there one day and took two boxes of paracetamol, I don't know if I wanted to die, I just couldn't handle the pain of loneliness anymore.

Knowing what I know now, it is pretty difficult to kill yourself with a couple of boxes of a paracetamol, but that 14 year old girl didn't know that, she thought it could end her life.

I took the pain killers and then lay down on my bed thinking I would just drift off, go to sleep and never wake up.

What then followed was just violent sickness, severe stomach cramps and illness for a few days, no one even knew what I had done. It was my little secret.

I actually enjoyed the pain back then and making myself sick, I felt like it was the only thing in my life I could control.

This became a theme in my life, not fitting in, feeling unworthy, self-harm, mostly in the way of eating unhealthily, late nights, drinking excessively and taking drugs.

I turned to drugs every weekend and became a party girl, when I was under the influence I had confidence, I could reinvent myself, I could be whoever I wanted to be, the life and soul of the party… Everyone wanted to be my friend, so I thought.

Because I was brushing my issues under the carpet though and masking them over the years my mental health just became even worse.

I became toxic, I was paranoid, insecure and destroyed many friendships and relationships because I couldn't stand the thought of anyone getting close to me and discovering the real me. They would find out, they would know I was different, that I didn't belong, and I wasn't worthy of their love.

I was terrified of being alone, but I create a huge chasm between myself and everyone I knew with my toxic energy which lead to me becoming even more alone. Oh, the irony.

A Fresh Start

Things in my life started to look up though when I was 29.

I got to the point where I had just had enough, enough of not being enough, enough of playing the victim, enough of a mundane life in a job that didn't bring me joy and in a city where I never felt at home or fit in.

I had just come out of a pretty toxic relationship, I had a good job, a lovely house, good friends but I wanted more. I didn't quite know what that was at that point, but I knew I wanted it and I was going to get it.

I had a family that lived in Jersey, not too far away, only an hour flight, but far enough away for me to start my life again.

I booked my flights that day, handed my notice in at my job, sold my car, everything in my home, all of my possessions and moved away to start my new life taking only one suitcase with me.

It's incredible the amount of crap that you accumulate over your lifetime! I mean how many clothes, shoes, books and just general shit does one person really need?

Throwing everything out just made me feel so free.

I felt like I could take on the world, I could achieve anything, this was the scariest thing I had ever done, starting again but the best decision I ever made.

It didn't last though, before long, my need to be loved and my insecurities came up again. I started looking for a new relationship which I entered into before I was ready, I rushed things and before I knew it, we were moving in together and I found out I was pregnant.

The joy I felt when I found out I was pregnant was like nothing I have ever experienced before, finally I would have someone to love me unconditionally, that I could be close to, that unbreakable bond.

I had such hopes and was filled with love, glowing, imagining what my baby would look like and who they would grow up to be.

But as I explained that was short lived.

The deep depths of depression surfaced again, the all-consuming dark thoughts. Terrible thoughts came and wouldn't leave me.

I couldn't do this, I was going to be a terrible mother, I wouldn't know how to love him, I didn't deserve his love; running through my mind on a daily basis. The pain became worse, my mobility became worse, I lost myself and I lost hope.

Who even was I? I didn't even know. I was a shell, completely empty, just waiting and wondering when this hell would end.

The midwives in the hospital must have become sick of me constantly in the hospital complaining. I didn't feel seen or understood, they see pregnant women every single day; I felt like I was just a number, a hypochondriac. Eventually though and I was offered an induction three weeks before my due date.

Yes!!!! Finally… Just get this baby out of me, I thought. I just need to sleep and to stop this never-ending pain.

I hadn't slept properly in months and spent my nights on the sofa for two months before giving birth.

What a big mistake that was though, I didn't know it was going to get worse, so much worse.

I didn't understand what was going on most of the time, the nurses using words I didn't understand, not explaining anything to me.

I had been in the hospital all day having taken the medication for the induction, waiting patiently for my baby to arrive.

I knew something was happening, I knew I was in labour, I mean a woman knows her own body, right?

But no one listened to me, I was told it was going to be a long time before my baby showed up and I should get some rest.

My partner was sent home and I was left alone, terrified and in pain.

This wasn't the pleasant experience I thought it was going to be, that was for sure. Fuck the natural route, I just wanted any drugs I could get my hands on.

No, gas and air doesn't work, just give me the hard stuff!

But I had to keep on asking, begging and begging to get some pain relief…

Only an hour after my partner left to go home my waters broke and up until that moment I had never experienced pain like that in my life.

I had bones fractured before, but nothing compared to this…

What the fuck was I thinking, why did I ever decide having a baby was a good idea, why did I insist on getting induced. Fuck, fuck, fuck…

Alone, in pain, terrified for my life and my baby's life.

Something wasn't right, I knew it wasn't, I just couldn't go on, I actually just wanted to die.

How can some women actually enjoy childbirth, I was thinking, how can they do this naturally?

From what I understand now doing research after the event, many women have reported that contractions after an induction are actually far more painful than contractions from a naturally induced labour.

Why wasn't this explained to me though? Why wasn't I given enough information about what could happen?

Nearly 24 hours after being in labour I had had enough, I was falling fast, I couldn't carry on, I had been crying and asking for an epidural, no idea how long for but finally I was given one and peace descended.

The pain stopped and I was numb. Finally, I was free and high as a kite, but no longer in pain.

Soon the contractions started to slow down though, the baby was distressed, he needed to come out.

No choice now but an emergency C-section. I will be honest with you I didn't have a fucking clue what was going on, I was delirious, didn't understand anything that was being told to me.

Scared my baby was going to die, that I was going to die, that it would all be my fault, I was wheeled into surgery.

I was to have surgery whilst being awake I was told and as I already had a drip epidural that would be sufficient for the pain, I am not sure what else they stuck in there I had no idea, maybe they added in some more morphine.

Then they started to cut, at first I couldn't feel anything still completely numb from the waist down but after the first few layers of tissue I could feel it.

The tearing of my insides, my flesh, I could feel everything.

I screamed & I begged for more painkillers but was told I had already had the maximum amount they could give me.

What the fuck was happening here? I was not supposed to be able to feel this. A human should never in their lives have to understand exactly what it feels like to have their stomach muscles torn apart.

I clearly have a low pain threshold I was told; I don't understand what happened or why it happened, but it happened, and I will forever have that memory engrained, lodged in my mind.

I certainly don't complain much about pain anymore now anyway.

Oh my fucking god this was lasting forever, where the fuck is my baby I thought. I just want him out.

Then nearly an hour of excruciating pain later and my baby boy was placed on me.

He wasn't crying, he was calm. His eyes were wide open, staring at me, they were blue. A deep, dark blue.

He was out, he was safe, and he was mine.

I was responsible for this tiny little human.

A huge sense of relief washed through me, he was alive, and he was safe.

I had no idea what to do with a baby, how to hold him, how to touch him but I would figure it out.

I knew without a shadow of a doubt that I would love this baby more than I had ever loved another human before. As cliché as it is, it is true, there is no love like a mother's love for her child.

I also knew that I would do anything to protect him and raise him to be brave, kind and intelligent.

I would make sure with everything I had that he would always feel loved and wanted and that no matter what I had to do; I would build a life that would make him proud. I would be a deserving mother.

But the magic disappeared, and I remembered the pain, I begged the anaesthetist to just put me under so I could sleep and not feel any more pain and off I went, down under into the abyss.

I don't know how much later I woke up but I was crying, scared, feeling alone and still in so much pain.

Two days after the birth in the hospital passed, pain, more pain, morphine, more pain, in a total daze.

I don't really remember much of it, if I am honest.

I remember being tired, confused and lonely.

I was high as a kite and left by myself with a newborn baby, like what the fuck was I supposed to do with him, I really didn't have a clue.

I wanted to breastfeed him, but I couldn't get him to latch, yet another thing I was failing at, I told myself.

Surely feeding your baby should come naturally to you and to your baby but it just wasn't happening. Guilt sank in, I gave him formula and I slept.

Then before I knew it I was taken off medication, made to get up and walk after being on an epidural for 2 days bed ridden and not having walked properly for a couple of months, whilst holding a crying baby who wanted feeding all the time.

Honestly, I felt like I was just part of a conveyor belt. OK, you've had your baby now, it's time to get out and go back home on your own.

I had just had major surgery and been through an incredibly traumatic experience, but I was treated like it was nothing. Like I just had to get on with it and get back to my normal life.

Everyone forgot about it, about the labour, about me, the focus was on the baby.

So, I had better just suck it up, I thought, and get on with it, push these feelings and confusion to one side and bury them, focus on looking after my baby.

Everyone said I was a natural mother, it looked like it came so easy to me, that I knew what I was doing but I really didn't have a clue.

Inside I was lost, scared and still in a lot of pain physically and mentally.

The months went on, I was trapped inside, where was I? Who was I? I had no idea.

No longer Emma Louise Hammond, now I was just Taylor's mum. No identity, no life, no hobbies, nothing… Just 'Mum'.

I hear a lot of mums struggle with losing their identity after having a child. This was true for me, I had no idea what to do with myself, how to think or how to be.

Every waking thought was consumed with him; Was he crying? Was he hungry? Was he breathing, even?

I was blessed with a baby that loved sleep, but could I sleep? Could I fuck! So terrified constantly that if I fell asleep, I would wake up and he wouldn't be there anymore.

Serious paranoia, sleep deprivation and depression.

Things took a turn for the worse though and my relationship with my partner ended.

On my own with a 5-month-old baby, what was I going to do, how would we survive?

He didn't understand though he just looked up at me with

his beautiful eyes always smiling and giggling. He was such a happy and calm baby. Even in the midst of a breakup and complete shake up of his life, he was secure, confident and full of love for me.

Wow, I must really be doing something right to have such an incredible, strong and happy baby.

He gave me the confidence to start again. I had to make it work, I had to survive on my own, I had to build an incredible life for him and make him proud.

It was such a tough period for me after becoming a single parent, still full of doubt about how I would make it work, I just knew that I would make it work.

I had to find somewhere to live, an affordable nursery, change my hours around at work and somehow work everything out so that we could afford to live and eat.

I worked my ass off and even had two jobs at one point, taking on an extra job in a bar a couple of nights a week but I was still barely scraping by.

Was this really what life was? Struggle after struggle, working hard and getting no reward, unhappiness and depression?

So, again in my life, I made a decision; I made the decision that I was in control of my destiny and that I would change my situation. It didn't matter where I was right now. I could rewrite my story; I could write a new book.

One where I had the power and I could create my reality however I wanted it and build the future I had always dreamed of. I was going to fulfil the promises I made to myself when I had my baby. I would make him proud.

Everything I ever needed was inside me all along, I just needed to strength to put it into action and not give up.

I had been looking into ways to make money online since my baby was born, I knew there was a better way, I just had to find it.

For the past 3 years since I became a single mother I have

been building businesses online, learning about social media marketing, digital marketing and how to sell products and services online without ever leaving my house.

Nearly two years ago I made the decision to set up and build my own business where I taught others to do the same.

At first my motivation was purely selfish, to provide for me and my family and give us a better life. But as I became stronger and an expert at growing my brand and delivering results for my clients, my motivation transformed.

I could help other parents, I could show them the steps I took to build my business and also support them in creating a lifestyle of freedom. One where they could work from home, spend more time with their children, have flexibility, travel more, experience more and not be weighed down with financial struggles.

A New Chapter

So where am I now? Over the last twelve months my business has completely transformed. I am completely self-employed, I choose my own hours to work, working no more than twenty hours a week. I have grown my business to a digital marketing and automation agency and have eight team members assisting me in delivering work to clients.

I am no longer worried about my finances and how to feed us, we can travel and go on holidays, but more importantly, I am happy and confident.

I can wake up every day now and embrace challenges, I am growing every single day as a person.

I know exactly who I am, and I continue to grow every single day.

My little boy is happy, intelligent, strong and confident. Just like his mother.

I am living proof that it doesn't matter what trauma you have suffered in your life, where you came from or what you have been through. That you have the power right inside you to shape your life however you want it. If you aren't happy, get up and change the channel.

All it takes is the decision to make a change.

★★★

Emma Hammond, AKA The Queen of Automation is a single mother living in Jersey, The Channel Islands.

After making the decision to build a better life for herself and her child, she threw herself into building a business around working two jobs, raising a child and battling with mental health issues.

Over a period of four months she increased her revenue in her business by over 900% all through organic marketing methods using Facebook and has never spent any money on advertising.

She works with service-based business owners helping them to create businesses that give them freedom and allows them to create their dream lives.

She also now runs her own agency that provides digital marketing & business process automation services.

Links to connect with Emma

Website – www.emmahammond.co.uk

Facebook – https://www.facebook.com/elhammond1

Facebook Group – https://www.facebook.com/groups/CreatingFreedomForEmpoweredBusinessOwners

Victoria

Having a baby is supposed to be the best feeling in the world. I have two young boys, but I can't tell you that about either of their births.

I'm going to tell you my experiences. They are not to frighten mums, put women off having children or give you nightmares, but because I have overcome these things and for years, I beat myself up about not getting it right.

When I found out I was pregnant with my first child I really did think 'oh shit'. It was a planned pregnancy, my hubby and I wanted a family, but I was scared. The thought of growing my baby and looking after myself wasn't a problem but the thought of giving birth scared me to death. I didn't make this known to others, after all, women give birth every day and I thought it was normal to be this scared.

Throughout the pregnancy we were constantly at the hospital as I had gestational diabetes and because I didn't want my baby to suffer because of this I was super controlling with what I ate, and I started losing weight. During my pregnancy I moved offices with my job which meant I was travelling an hour to work each day on the motorway.

I should maybe give you some background here as I think it didn't help me and how I felt at this time. I didn't live near my family, I didn't like my job and at this point I was being bullied at work. I didn't really have any friends as I had moved away from where I had grown up and found it hard to make friends as I went to work and home and that was about it.

I moved to a new office hoping for a new start. The people were lovely. I had training in my new role, but I began to have horrific nightmares. I would wake up in the night crying, sobbing so hard that my pillow was wet. I dreamt about being in a car accident on the motorway and there was blood everywhere. I could see it and hear the sounds so vividly and I was so scared that my baby would be hurt. I got so scared about driving and hurting my baby that it impacted on my ability to drive, and therefore, travel to work. I was signed off work as it affected me so badly that all the stress I was putting myself under had given me high blood pressure.

I thought I would be ok now as I was safe at home and didn't have to drive, but I wasn't. I had just cut myself off from the world as I spent all day alone in the flat with no friends, nowhere to go, so all I could do was worry. I tried to distract myself with getting our home 'baby ready' and this worked for a little while, but I was never far away from nightmares or being frightened about the birth of our son.

When I was 7 months pregnant, I was told that my baby was 'cherubic' because of my gestational diabetes and the baby getting too much sugar. Again, I was even more closely monitored, and more appointments followed. I was scared. I was frightened that I had this large sick baby inside me that I had done this to because of my bad habits and lifestyle. My consultant said I would not be allowed to reach 40 weeks gestation because of my baby having a large head.

I was not blooming. I was very good at pretending I was though. I got up each day and did all the things I needed to do and went to bed each night. As I lay in the quiet or was there in the daytime my thoughts roamed to 'I've got to get this baby out, I'm not strong enough, how am I going to do this?'. 'I'm not good enough' became my mantra, which ultimately became 'how am I going to be a Mum?'

I was given a tour of the hospital I had chosen, and hubby and I walked around the maternity unit. It didn't make me feel any better as we were shown the midwife led units, with baths and beds, music, dimmed lighting and tv's and then were told we would not be able to have our baby here as I had a high risk pregnancy. So, we were taken along to a crowded maternity ward and a very clinical looking maternity suite. My hubby and I came out and both commented on the 'here's what you could have won' tour verses that what I was going to have. I had always imagined a water birth but very early on I was told that I would be in the maternity suite because of my diabetes.

I couldn't do anything about this. I just took on more awful thoughts and didn't settle at all. I should say that my hubby was very supportive, he did the early morning shopping trips for hash browns and fizzy orange and was by my side at all appointments. I still felt lonely, especially when he had to go to work and as I didn't have many friends, I became a friend with my TV and a detective programme called 'Poirot'. These programmes kept me entertained and that's how I spent my time in the last few weeks.

The week before I was due to be induced, I was given a sweep at the hospital. That night I had pains in my tummy and a few minor contractions, but it all stopped, and nothing further happened. Hubby and I were in our own home and I remember wishing so hard that my labour would start that night so I wouldn't have to be induced. I was so upset everything had stopped, but I joked that our son was obviously too comfy to move right now.

The following Wednesday I was taken into hospital. The Friday nights movements had left me just 1cm dilated so I was given a pessary to start the induction process. Once again, I wished it would happen naturally, but nothing did. Hubby stayed with me the whole time I was in the hospital during the days and then it was time for him to leave. I didn't want him to leave me there alone on the ward, but he wasn't allowed to stay and went home for the night. That night I didn't sleep. The ward was really busy with women in and out as they came into the ward and then left for the maternity suite to have their babies. Some women were noisily sucking on gas and air, others were screaming and panting, and I had nurses monitoring baby and me, and taking my blood sugars through the night. When hubby arrived the next morning, I was tired, stressed and I just wanted to go home. I was examined and our son still wasn't moving of his own accord, so I was given another sweep. I had two monitors on, one for me and one for baby. My blood sugars were taken throughout the day but again nothing happened, and I didn't get any nearer to going to the maternity suite.

Again, my hubby left for the night and I was alone again. The ward was really busy, and no one had really updated us as to what would be happening. When would we be going to the maternity suite? And indeed, we had no real knowledge of what was happening next. I had been told that I would probably be taken to be induced on Thursday if the pessary and sweep hadn't worked but they hadn't, and here I was still on the ward with no one updating me. As it came time for lights out, I tried to sleep but again the ward was a hive of activity with everyone else except me. Again, I didn't sleep and was getting very upset. Eventually I was told by a nurse that because of urgent cases that had come in that day I had been moved to the next day's list. I totally understood that as baby and I seemed to be ok and he was certainly not budging at that time, but after 48 hours of no sleep I was a tired and emotional wreck. I didn't want to be induced, I hated the thought of the clinical room and not knowing what would happen to me or how I would feel.

The next morning, I was taken into the delivery room. I was so scared. I didn't know what was going to happen, I didn't like not being in control of myself and my body and I think this is how things got really crazy.

My waters were broken, and I was given gas and air. This made me laugh so much. I was hooked up to a drip for my diabetes and a monitor was put on to our son's head. I was put onto a bed and couldn't move. I was unable to go for a wee myself and had to have my bladder opened by the midwife which was really unnatural. Then the midwife explained that because I was induced that things can get pretty painful really quickly so I might want to think about pain relief. At this particular point I was quite happy on gas and air, but I was frightened. I didn't think I could handle the pain and I didn't know how on earth I was going to manage to get my cherubic son out. So, out of blind panic I said yes to the pain relief and was given diamorphine, and this is where things went really wrong for me. I very rarely take any pain killers, not even paracetamol, and I had never used any drugs of any sort.

The diamorphine completely knocked me out of it. I was sick, I was so tired through lack of sleep that I was emotional and now couldn't even see straight. I couldn't hear what people were saying to me and thankfully dipped in and out of sleep for a while. I had lost myself. I had lost control of me, and this scared me more than anything else ever had. I was told I could have an epidural now and agreed even though I was unsure, but I couldn't voice my concerns. I don't remember being in that much pain, but I thought I would not be able to cope without it.

It took a while for the anaesthetist to come and chat about the epidural and then to complete the procedure. I have no idea what he said to me, or how on earth I signed or said anything to give my consent. The diamorphine had made me feel awful, but the worst part was feeling dizzy, sick, lost and just not me at all. I couldn't comprehend and respond to what the midwife was saying to me, but I know I wanted to scream, 'Stop, I don't want this anymore. I have lost control of everything; I don't feel like myself anymore and I don't want to have my baby like this'. But I couldn't.

I was in labour for hours, 19 exactly. Day turned to night and midwives changed. I had three different midwives; I think. My hubby chatted to them and knew their names and how long they'd been midwives, but I didn't have a clue.

Finally, I got the message that I was 10 cm dilated. I could sense that the midwife was keen to try and get me to push but I couldn't feel anything, my body was numb, and my mind was spinning.

'Right', said the midwife, 'the next time you feel a contraction you need to push – Ok?' Erm, No. What is a contraction? What does a contraction feel like? What am I supposed to be feeling? I started to panic. I remember crying because I was scared, but also because I couldn't feel anything, either physically or mentally. The midwife realised that I didn't know what was happening as she started to shout at me to push when the monitor showed I was having a contraction.

What did I need to do to push? I couldn't feel my body… I didn't know if I was pushing or not. I was tired, I was sick, and I was scared. I couldn't do this anymore. I began to get really upset and the midwife now had to try and calm me down, but I knew she wasn't happy as she kept looking at my little boy's heart rate and he had begun to get distressed. They needed to get him out now.

My little room suddenly became full of different staff and a doctor. The doctor said that they could help get baby out with forceps, but this made the situation worse as I had read so many awful stories about forceps that my midwife had to calm me down again. I agreed to ventouse, but I don't think the doctor had done this procedure before in a real-life situation. I was a mess, but somewhere in this crazy scene the doctor had managed to get the ventouse attached to my son's head. I don't remember feeling anything; no contractions, no pain, no baby and not my body either. Somehow, I managed at the last minute, with a doctor, ventouse and my midwife telling me when to push, to get my son out, but not without an episiotomy.

I don't remember the moment our eldest son was born, I don't recall hearing him cry for the first time, I don't know if I got to hold him or what anyone said. I remember being sewn up. I remember being told to take a shower. I remember that my room was now empty and all I could see everywhere were bloody tissues, towels, bedding and blankets.

I took a shower on my own, my head was still fuzzy, and I was washing blood off me. My back hurt, my legs were wobbly, and I thought 'thank God, that is over'.

Back in the maternity suite, I was told there was no room for us on the maternity ward so we would have to stay there in another room. The side room was so hot. We shared the room with another woman who had a little girl and there was just a baffle board between us for privacy. Hubby was told to go home and get some rest. I was tired, everything ached, and I was swollen all over because I had had to sit on the bed in the same position for around 18 hours. My little boy was with me but every time I tried to put him down in his cot he cried. So, I sat up with him for the rest of the night with him lying in my swollen arms, frightened that I was going to drop him because my head was fuzzy, I was dehydrated, and I was so tired. Because we were in the delivery suite when I tried to come out of the room to ask for help, I was told to go back in as I wasn't allowed to be wandering about. No one came to see us. I didn't know what I was supposed to do. I didn't know if I was supposed to try and feed my son and I didn't have anything to feed him with. Yes, I have boobs. But my boobs were not leaking or swollen with milk and I had no idea how to breastfeed. Eventually I was able to ask a midwife to bring me a little bottle of baby milk in case my son was thirsty, but he didn't really take any, but this made me anxious for him as the room was so hot.

I text my hubby and asked him to come back, that I needed help. I just wanted some support, but I was left alone all night. Hubby arrived at about 7 am to an emotional, crying mess. I was feeling sick from the drugs, sore from the drips, monitors, epidural and from sitting in one place the previous day when in labour and at night holding my son so he could sleep. I hadn't slept for three days and had no idea what I was supposed to do now. I remember finally being visited by a midwife who told me the breast-feeding nurse would be along to see me and also that our son had jaundice and they would need to take a blood sample. This was horrendous. The nurse battled to squeeze blood out of my sons' foot, and he was screaming. I was so stressed and upset. After everything I had been through, I just know that in this moment I could have torn the midwife apart with my bare hands because she was hurting my son.

The breastfeeding nurse came and tried to help me to breastfeed, but my son wouldn't latch on and then when he did, there was nothing there. My boobs had no milk at this point, but I was told to keep trying. In the afternoon my Mum and Dad came to visit, and we were still in this awful, hot, tiny and inappropriate room on the birthing suite. I was tired, hot and irritated so I just cried, and my dad took my hubby out to get a burger and to do something useful.

Finally, we were moved onto the maternity ward. Hubby was with me and we were visited by his parents. I couldn't talk to them, I just sat and cried. We were told that our son would need to be under a heat lamp to help with his jaundice, so one was brought next to my bed but every time I tried to put him in it he cried, so I kept picking him up. The tests showed his kidneys were fine, he just needed to kick the jaundice. I was still not producing any milk, so we were feeding our son with formula to keep fluid flushing through him. After Steven went home, I fed and changed our son. When I went to put him down, he was really upset so I asked midwife for help. She was really short with me and told me I needed to wind James and left. I had no idea how to do this. I had no experience of little children in my family or within our group of friends. I had to buzz again for the midwife because my son wouldn't stop crying. The midwife appeared after a little while and showed me how to put him over my shoulder and rub his back to help him. Ok, I can do that I thought. Finally, he burped, and I was able to settle him. He was naked with a cover over his eyes and under a heat lamp next to my bed. He was not happy there, so I moved him closer to me and held his hand all night and sang to him. Another sleepless night for me but I was desperate to get my son out of the hospital. I asked the midwife for some formula to feed my son in the early hours of the morning, she told me to try and breast feed. I didn't know how. My boobs weren't leaking, they weren't big and full of milk, but I tried. The midwife pinched and squeezed my boobs until I was sore, I had a blood blister on one of my boobs and my son still wasn't latching on properly. I was so upset as this is what I was supposed to do, wasn't it? The midwife told me that I would never breast feed my son if I didn't try. She did bring me the formula as my son needed fluid to help with his jaundice, but I cried, and I felt totally inadequate. I had not been able to feel or experience the birth of my son and now I couldn't feed him either.

The next morning Steven came back at 7 am and we moved the baby's bed next to the window to help him get the sunlight. James wouldn't settle under the lamp so they brought a glow blanket that I could wrap him up in and hold him whilst it tried to help his jaundice. More blood tests were done, we fed him, clothed him and sat with him under the window in the daylight as much as possible. It was now Sunday evening and we were told that we might be able to go home soon if the latest blood tests didn't show any kidney problems. About 8.30pm we were told that we could go home as his jaundice was slightly better and his blood test was fine. The problem was that we did not foresee that we would not be able to breastfeed, so we had no formula milk at home. So, before we could go home Hubby had to go to a late-night pharmacy the other side of Manchester to buy formula milk. And I waited in the hospital with my little one. Over an hour later he appeared with milk and all I wanted to do was run out of there and never return. I had had an awful experience. The hospital was overcrowded, some midwives had not been helpful or sympathetic at all and I needed to be back to myself and in control. So, at about 10pm on that Sunday night we left the hospital. My son had not been given a bath and we had not been shown how to bathe him, so he still was messy and had blood stuck in his hair, but we wanted to take him away… somewhere safe.

My hubby drove so slowly that night. I think he thought our son would break. We got home to our flat, sat our sleeping son down in the middle of the living room floor in his car seat and looked at each other and said, 'what do we do now?' I said we have a cup of tea, go to bed and then just do what we need to do. So, we did.

The next day a fabulous community midwife visited us at home. She was sad at hearing what I had gone through, organised for me to have painkillers and medicine to help me go to the loo without harming my stitches and told me that if I wanted to try breastfeeding, she would help me and first I just needed to massage my boobs when I get a bath and see if they begin to leak any milk. So, I did this, but they didn't. When she came back the next day, she taught my hubby and I how to bath our son. She helped us get all the blood out of his hair and we were grateful for her time and her patience. I explained that my boobs were sore, and I was stressed so she said it was ok for me to use formula as lots of mums do, as some women can't breast feed for a number of reasons. I felt better but still like I'd failed. I just then took one feed after another, one day after another, and I was a mum to our son. He was happy and healthy and that was all that mattered.

For years after I had my son I suffered with depression. I blamed myself for everything that wasn't right and perfect in his birth and how I couldn't breastfeed. I was permanently sad, and this was ruining my relationship with my son and my hubby. I did go and see a doctor after a while, but I refused to take antidepressants and wasn't given anything else as an option. So, I fought it myself for a long time. I had days where I didn't go out. Days where I couldn't get dressed. Days where I was washed, dressed and out the house by 8.30am and I had cleaned my house from top to bottom too. I was happier when my son was asleep because I could watch tv and eat chocolate. I love my son, but this was so tough. I quit my job after my maternity leave. Spent time with my son out walking and trying to do all the things I should be doing but I was too scared to go to any mum groups. Eventually I decided I needed to find a part time job so I was away from my son for some time each week and also, so we could earn a bit more money. I did. I worked 3 days a week and found a fantastic childminder for James. I started working a lot, but I enjoyed the time I had with James more now. We moved house, I started power walking, I increased my hours at work and things felt better. I was still so sad but berated myself for feeling like this. Finally, I saw my GP and was told I could go for some CBT if I didn't like the idea of taking medication. I did. My therapist was lovely, and I saw her every couple of weeks for over a year. Things felt better and life got better. I still felt like I was cheated out of the birth of my son and that I was a failure for not being able to breastfeed, but the nightmares were gone. I was able to sleep at night and I was able to reconcile how I felt.

I love my eldest son and even went on to have another little boy (I love him too). That is a whole other story. I am a very lucky Mummy and my sons are the most loving, kind and super funny boys. My hubby and I have been through A LOT, but we are still here and have celebrated 10 years of marriage this year. What would I change from this experience – well, I wouldn't take the drugs, but more than that is I would encourage mums to believe in themselves. Have the courage to follow your heart and your intuition. Talk to people about how you feel and if you need help to ask. If I had of done these things sooner, then I think my life would have been less stressful and my depression would not have been so bad for so long. I hope if you're reading this that it isn't too bleak. I had a rubbish time but there were so many circumstances that led to this that were outside my control.

I am very lucky to be a mum. I am here and I survived. I have heard too many birth trauma stories and I wish it was something that didn't happen anymore. The fact is that being pregnant and giving birth is a huge deal. We just need to take care of ourselves and each other a bit more. I love being a mum to my boys; they are the best things to ever happen to me. Life is good.

★★★

Victoria Coupe lives in Manchester, UK, with her husband and two young boys. She works part time and also runs a group for Mums to support each other and to find help and advice when they need it.

Mums in Mind
www.mumsinmind.org
mumsinmindorg@gmail.com
Community Group:
www.facebook.com/groups/728340797336174
Page:
www.facebook.com/MumsinMind

Lola

All through your child bearing years everyone tells you every pregnancy is different, yet during my fourth pregnancy every medical professional would mention how this birth was going to be a breeze as my other three labours were near on perfect from a medical stand point; how wrong could everyone have been. I decided to tell my story, not as closure for me as I don't believe that is a possibility, the memories and after-effects will never be gone, but I decided to tell my story in the hope that medical professionals and well-wishing friends and family will not disregard the fact that every pregnancy and labour is different and it doesn't matter how many labours you have had, it doesn't get any easier and the risks are just the same; anyone can suffer a birth trauma even if it is your first or tenth baby and each experience is relevant.

I started having children very young; I was seventeen when my first daughter came into the world. Her pregnancy was perfect, no major issues. Medically, she was two days late by my calculations; she came on her due date within forty-four minutes of my waters breaking. Thirty-three minutes of pushing and my daughter came into the world without pain relief, I had a three pronged tear resulting in one-hundred-and-forty-six stitches both externally and internally but in all honesty, I thought that this was just how childbirth was, I thought stitches were part and parcel and her birth went well.

Four years later we found we were expecting again, and

this pregnancy again went without any issues. This time we were five days overdue when she arrived by the doctors reckoning, but on her due date or there abouts by ours (we are sure our drunken 21st birthday holiday to Portugal was to blame for her arrival). The labour was slightly longer than the first but at ten to six in the morning our little girl graced us with her presence. The delivery of the placenta was where everything went downhill. As usual, the midwife injected into my thigh and I sat back thinking I had at least ten minutes before the final part of this labour would be over, how wrong was I. The midwife had just removed the needle from my thigh before she started tugging at the cord, snapping it. She proceeded by trying to drag the placenta out, snapping the whole of the cord that was available outside my body. I was confused; I didn't remember this being part of the procedure the first time; I remembered it being an injection, some gentle pushing on your stomach, deep breathing and a push or two, before it flopped out. The midwife moved from the bed and went to the instruments placed in a row on a trolley towards the back of the room, she returned with forceps. Before I could even ask what they were for, she was pulling at bits of skin within my private area, pulling and yanking what she could, trying to grasp any bit of cord she could find. The pain was excruciating, and I was screaming at my husband to help me and get her off me. My husband is a very quiet man and for the first time in our five-year relationship, I remember him bellowing at the top of his voice, "Can't you see you're hurting her?!" The midwife stood back in shock as if she was offended by his tone, "I don't need to put up with this!" she replied and left the room. Both bewildered and exhausted I fell asleep, my husband slept across a table in the delivery suite, three hours passed, and a new midwife came in. She said, "Have you been able to pass water?" My reply was, "Did they get all of the placenta out?!" She looked at me horrified and frantically grabbed the notes from the end of the bed and ran out the room, returning with a surgeon. "We are going to have to manually remove the placenta, but first we need to take some bloods and find a surgical room and team to sort this out." I remember wondering why they were so worried, I managed to sit up and look at myself in a mirror; my eyes were yellow, my skin was yellow, and I didn't look well at all. They took bloods and half an hour later came back with the results. "You are showing first signs of toxic shock syndrome and we need to put you on a course of intravenous antibiotics and fluids and get you into theatre." I was strapped up to drips and wheeled into a theatre room, a lovely Chinese nurse came in and sat at the top end of the bed where my head was and started to stroke my head, telling me I was going to be fine and it would be over soon. The next thing I knew, I was asleep. I woke up on a ward, baby and daddy sat next to me, and it was the first time I could actually inspect our newborn daughter. She was perfect in every way. We spent seven nights in the hospital, leaving feeling well, like nothing had happened. What we didn't know was that this incident was going to curse us in a year or two.

A year and a half later we found we were pregnant again; we were using contraception but obviously the powers that be decided we needed to introduce a third child into our world.

With all my pregnancies I have always 'just known' when we were expecting and this time was no different, we were unsure of how far along we were due to the contraception but we assumed it was definitely early, maybe two or three weeks, so as we came round to the thought of having three small children and the weeks passed, we eagerly awaited the 12-week scan date. The date was booked for Monday the 14th December 2009; on the Friday I began to feel unwell, like I had the flu with slight cramping, which I assumed to be the uterus stretching and things moving into place. On the Saturday I noticed a tiny bit of dark blood on a visit to the bathroom and called the early pregnancy unit, who told me it was nothing to worry about; they told me it was quite normal as it was old blood. By Sunday morning I really didn't feel well, and the bleeding was slightly heavier. My gut feeling was to get checked over. I made my way to A&E who took my temperature, blood pressure, and the usual bits but said they couldn't send me for a scan as they weren't open on Sundays, and as I was booked in the next day I would just have to wait.

I made my way home and by the time I reached home I had what I could only describe as a fever, I was shaking as if I was freezing, yet felt like my head would blow off with the heat. I put myself to bed. I was asleep for a few hours when I was woken up by a pain in my back, I took myself to the bathroom and as I went to sit down on the toilet I was doubled over in pain.

As I looked down there was a flood of blood all down my legs and over the floor. I was screaming in pain. There were bits of body tissue over my feet. I let out a mighty groan and out came our baby.

I screamed uncontrollably, sobbing so hard I couldn't breathe, I didn't even know what to do. My husband came to see what had happened; I slammed the bathroom door; there was no need for both of us to have to endure this dramatic scene.

I wrapped the baby up in tissue and put it inside a sandwich bag, inside a rucksack, as I made my way to the hospital. When we got there, we were rushed into a side room and I handed over the package to a nurse who said they would dispose of it. I was so exhausted both physically and emotionally, I just nodded. They arranged to give me a scan. "There is no baby", the sonographer said, as if I didn't already know. "Give it a few weeks and you can try again", and we were ushered out the hospital and it was never spoken of again. We later received a letter to say we were in fact 21-weeks pregnant at the time and that during the scans they saw I had a severely damaged womb due to blunt force trauma that had left a huge amount of internal scarring. I was later told by my GP they believed this to be due to the placental removal attempt by the midwife at my last birth and didn't think I would be able to carry a baby term again without medical intervention.

Three months later we found out we were expecting again, and as you can imagine, we made sure I was wrapped up in cotton wool. We successfully made it to term. We found out we were expecting our first son which made the previous loss a little easier as without it we wouldn't have a son. The day I went into labour with our son I couldn't sleep, I was up watching a documentary at 6am when my waters broke. I was experiencing no pain at all, so I walked upstairs and told my husband my waters had broken and to rest until I was ready to leave. At 9am we decided to make our way to the hospital. We got there and I was checked over to be told I was only 5cm dilated and should go home. I asked if they could find me a room as due to a loss I didn't want to risk my labour progressing fast without medical support, I had also been having nightmares my son would be stillborn for the last few months so felt an urge to be at the hospital. There was one room with a birthing pool, and I was asked if I wanted to have a water birth. As I intended it to be my last, I thought why not?! They advised it took at least half an hour to fill, but not to worry because the baby wouldn't arrive before then. He did.

My son's birth was the most tranquil and medically hands-off experience ever. My son was born to the Boney M song, 'Mary's Boy Child', and was born in the most magical and relaxed way you could imagine. He was born on Monday the 13th December 2010 at 12.15pm, a year to the day of my miscarriage. We were home by 2pm that same day.

For seven years, we went along happily with our two daughters and our son. I was on the contraceptive coil (or Intrauterine device (IUD)) and it now needed to be changed, so I decided to go down the sterilisation route. I was told even if I wanted to move forward with it, I would have to wait a few months before a surgery slot would be available, which I was fine with. I went on the contraceptive pill and waited for my surgery date. Then we found out we were expecting…

We weren't prepared for this. We finally felt we were getting a bit of freedom back; we had a seven-year-old, a ten-year-old and a fourteen-year-old, all in school; we didn't want to start that baby phase again. We looked into our options but ultimately we knew with all we had been through, each child was a blessing and if we were meant to have four, so be it…

Then the bleeding started…

I knew the signs…

On Christmas Day, as I cooked dinner for my whole family, I lost another of our children. I kept a brave face on, smiled as the children opened their presents, cried and blamed the onions, went into my room to sob silently into my pillow while Christmas EastEnders was on, asking, 'Why us? Not once but twice?!'

We decided obviously this was what was meant to happen and that maybe we were done having kids and to enjoy all the freedom we could, so being the people we were we decided we were going to go out on our first New Year's Eve ever. We arranged a babysitter and went and had a great night out. People may not understand how after only a week of losing a child you can go out, but to be honest it was a good distraction, I could just be me and my husband could just be him, not mummy and daddy, just *us*.

Every few days I would take pregnancy tests as the doctor suggested; they couldn't push my sterilisation until I got a negative test... We still didn't have a negative result by my husband's birthday in mid-January; we couldn't understand why a negative hadn't appeared yet as my hCG levels had dropped enough to miscarry. So, we went to the early pregnancy unit for a scan, to be told that there was a pregnancy developing but no embryo could be seen... The doctors were as confused as us and I had to return a week later; still, a thickened womb with no embryo, so we had blood tests that confirmed I was pregnant. The doctors said if they couldn't see anything at the next scan they would determine it a pregnancy of unknown location and I would have to take medication to expel the womb thickening. The next week we went for a scan and there flickering on the screen was a heartbeat, a 6-week-old little embryo on the screen, as clear as day.

This left us all, including the medical staff, in a state of confusion; it couldn't be a twin of the miscarried baby or the same baby as I would have been 12-weeks. This was a new pregnancy, and the doctor said in astonishment, "You fell pregnant a week after your miscarriage." ... New Year's Eve.

The pregnancy went pretty well, there just seemed to be a lot of confusion about our due date. First the 25th September, then the 7th October, they finally they settled on the 11th October. Throughout the pregnancy I was told, "It's baby number four, you know what you're doing, it should be easy." I think it gave me a bit of a sense of a false security, plus the fact my last full-term pregnancy's labour went so beautifully, surely this was going to be just as perfect.

The 7th of October came and went, as well as the 11th of

October, and no medical staff seemed to be at all concerned. My anxiety was through the roof by the 17th of October; I went to the midwife and said I was concerned as we were already six days overdue by their scan calculations (I did try to explain I have large babies so this shouldn't have been used as a factor) but yet, ten days overdue by my dates and with the past experience of retained placenta etc I wanted to get this labour moving. The midwife offered me a sweep, and if nothing developed, to go in for induction on the 20th. I took the sweep as this had been successful with my second daughter, so I was holding out the same hope. Nothing happened. On the morning of the 20th, my husband rang the labour ward and they had no beds available, so we had to call back every hour to see if there was a bed available. After four 4 hours I'd had enough; I picked up my suitcase and said to my husband I was going to the hospital and not leaving until I had had the baby. We arrived at the hospital to be left in the waiting room for a further two hours, then we were finally given a bed. I remember thinking no one was really telling us anything, I'd never been induced before and had no idea what to expect and every time I asked a question, I was spoken to like I was being stupid and they kept referring to the fact this was my fourth baby and I should know, like I was some kind of labour expert.

At 10pm they came to my bed and told my husband he had to leave, and they would be giving me a pessary at some point during the night. When my husband asked if they would call him should the labour progress, knowing my history of fast progression, he was looked at as if he had insulted the midwife's mother.

At 1.45am a midwife woke me up to give me some paracetamol and insert the pessary, I silently prayed that it would progress slowly, and it would kick off after 8am when my husband could come back. 8am came around and there was no progression. My husband asked a nurse what the next step was, she informed him that if nothing had happened by this evening, they would burst my waters at around lunchtime. My waters went and I told the head midwife, who said, "No, they haven't. I would know if they had, as you would be in pain!" So, it seemed to me, I was an expert when it suited them, but I was not clever enough to figure out my waters had broken. I explained to the midwife that I have a high pain threshold as I've had three children without any pain relief, so not everyone is a screaming banshee when they are in labour. She wasn't impressed.

At 3pm a doctor came to do the ward rounds and asked me if my waters had gone, and before the words could leave my mouth, the head midwife butted in and said no, so he proceeded to get the instruments ready to burst my waters. I protested and said that I was sure they had, and his reply was, "Well, I will be the judge of that!" He proceeded to attempt to burst my waters, and with a hand up my vagina, he turned to me and said, "Oh. It appears they have gone."

An hour passed and still nothing had progressed, so the decision was made to move me to the delivery suite and hook me up to the hormone drip. A midwife came in and proceeded to prep my hand to insert the drip. As she inserted the drip into my right hand, I passed out. As I came around the drip was now in my left hand and she handed me a glass of water and put it down to exhaustion.

They put the drip on to level 1 and I wasn't having any contractions, so it was decided to put it on to level 2. This brought on irregular contractions and I was asked if I wanted pain relief, which I declined. I kept thinking, 'it's fine, it will soon be over'. I was actually quite hyped up, like a fighter, before a match; I was ready to get this over with. The midwife decided that maybe moving the bed would be helpful, so the bed was moved up to the point I was basically in a seated position using my elbows to keep myself from slipping off the bed that was now vertical.

Then, I was informed that I'd had the drip put up to the last level. I had never felt pain like it. I lost my vision; all I could hear was people talking and I begged for gas and air. I was given the gas and air and I gulped it down as much as I could as it was the only thing taking the edge off the pain, but it wasn't lasting long enough, so I was gulping faster and harder making me more high. At one point, I felt as if I was on the ceiling of the room and everyone was beneath me; it was the most surreal experience. The contractions were continuous pain, not what I was used to at all; previously, my contractions had always been like peaks and troughs, allowing a few seconds grace until the next one; this was like continuous pain. I remember thinking to myself 'this is how people die of pain'. Was I going to die?

My husband begged them to give me an epidural; even though it was against what I had wanted, he could see this was something I had never experienced before. He later told me, I was telling him I didn't want to die, and that this was going to kill me, I have no recollection of that.

The anaesthetist came in, I couldn't tell you what she looked like as I was still blind by the pain, I just remember her saying she couldn't issue an epidural while I was in this state and that a C-section may be an option at this point. I remember saying, "Yes! Get him out! I don't care, get him out!" The surgeon was called in and they decided to check how far dilated I was. At this point, I was only 5cm and I was now begging that they cut him out. All of a sudden, the sudden urge to push came over me. I told them I needed to push! They were screaming at me, "NO! NO! You will kill this baby if you do!" I was so afraid; I didn't know what was happening and the natural urge came over me, but I didn't want to kill my baby. A midwife who was in charge of monitoring the baby's heart rate screamed, "There's no heartbeat!" A doctor put his hand up inside me, and as he pulled his hand out, there was blood everywhere. He turned to my husband and said, "Pull that emergency cord now!" My husband pulled it and ran out of the room, which was filled with ten new people at this point. I have no recollection of how my son was born as my heart failed and I had to be resuscitated. My mum, who was in the room, said the baby was born floppy and unresponsive, and was attended to while doctors worked on me.

My husband had gone into the hallway and called his mum. He asked her to come to the hospital as he had lost his new baby and thought he was going to lose his wife too.

When I came around, my son was still on the observation table, thankfully healthy, but the room resembled something from a horror movie; there was blood everywhere, up the walls, all over me, even in my hair and on my face. Once I had got my bearings, I held my son for the first time; he was perfect, no one would have known he had such an experience entering the world.

Silently, in the corner of the room, a midwife was writing up the birth notes. Whilst people were in the room, she never said a word, yet as soon as people had left, she wanted to explain why things had gone the way they did.. I said to her, "Do not say anything until my husband is here", as I didn't feel I was coherent, and I was still processing what had happened, whilst adjusting to the instant reality of a newborn. She wasn't happy with this response and stormed out of the room. We were left for hours in a blood-soaked room, to the point we got our stuff together and walked out with our baby; no one batted an eyelid, it took them six hours to even realise we had left.

Over the first couple of weeks of my youngest son's life, I felt disconnected, trying to think about what had happened and why it didn't sit right with me that this was just a bad birth experience, so I went to my doctor who explained to me that I had experienced a traumatic birth, and an unnecessary one at that.

Firstly, no one is supposed to go to the third level of the hormone drip without adequate pain relief, as it can send the body into shock and lead to heart failure. The fact that I was seventeen days overdue, as someone with my history and the damage from my previous labours, shouldn't have been allowed. The doctors examining me without permission has a name – 'medical abuse', and that is also not allowed. Since my birth I have been diagnosed with PTSD and have an unhealthy obsession with having my children with me, as I don't trust any authority figure with their safety, and I have also got physical injuries still occurring two years later, including lack of feeling in my hand from where the drip was put in incorrectly causing permanent nerve damage. Also, due to my body going into shock, I now have nervous system issues that I will never recover from. My doctor has helped me to compile a complaint that is being taken to court, the problem is that the hospital has 'lost' my notes meaning it is my word against theirs, which adds insult to injury.

I want to add that my births have occurred at two separate London hospitals, so this is negligence on a wider scale than just a certain hospital. I decided to share my story, so women out there know that it's OK to feel that something they have experienced was wrong and can be voiced without fear of reprisal. I have been told by members of my family I should thank myself lucky I can't recollect everything and should get over it; that doesn't make it easier, it actually makes it harder as all you can do is try to piece together what you can remember and hope that your memories are not false.

I want to add that writing this story has helped to heal, as

I have been able to put my thoughts to paper and share my experience without judgement; no one reading this will judge me or feel my story is me being over dramatic, as if you have written in this book or you're reading this book, it is because you also feel the need to heal and in a strange and magical way, that bonds us all.

A feeling of violation is not you being dramatic, a fear of death is not you being dramatic and a belief that your birth did not go well is not dramatic; these are all reasonable fears and you are within your rights to feel them and do not let anyone with a medical degree or otherwise tell you differently.

Also, it is OK to let yourself heal in any way you see fit; meditation, therapy, medication or writing, these are all valid ways to allow yourself to heal and none of it is attention seeking.

I beg you to find your peace and I send my love to you whilst you do, the road is rocky with twists and turns, but the destination is so worth it.

★★★

Baby Lola 13/12/09 and Baby Ruby 25/12/16
Two diamonds gained in heaven,
Two angels picked too soon,
Two babies loved forever
Live among the stars and moon.

★★★

Lola Lunn hails from South London, and is a mother of 4, married to her childhood sweetheart of 16 years.

Lola is a social influencer who goes under then name 'The Spiritual Gangster', known for her down to earth portrayal of accepting spirituality without any BS. Lola has a large spiritual

following on her blog, 'The Celestial Child'.
Lola is currently studying a degree in creative writing at Birkbeck University London, and is also the author of Amazon #1 top seller, 'The Day The Phoenix Rose', with more books to come in the series; Lola is currently working on a range of fiction and nonfiction, and starting an online writers community, "The Relentless Scribblers Society", which can also be found on Facebook.
All her details can be found on www.LolaLunn.com

Michelle

As I child I remember changing my dream career constantly. First, I would be a doctor, then a lawyer, marine biologist and whatever else my mind decided. But my heart has always desired being a mother. There was never any doubt that I wanted to be a mom. However, when I was 19 that privilege was almost taken away from me. At 18 I was diagnosed with cervical dysplasia which in layman's terms means that I had pre cervical cancer. If left untreated the abnormal cells on my cervix would turn cancerous. In smaller amounts they leave the cells to see if they go away on their own, but because of the amount that I had, I needed surgery.

I had woken up from my surgery groggy and sore. A lovely nurse came in to check my vitals and to bring me some toast and orange juice. As I began to nibble on my toast my OBGYN came in to tell me how it went. It was then I was told that they removed more of my cervix than they anticipated, so much so that if I were to carry children it wouldn't be full term as I wouldn't have enough lining in my cervix to hold the baby. I felt that my world had ended, something that I wanted more than anything in this world was potentially taken away from me. Although I was grateful that they caught it in time before it got worse, I felt that my one job, that only a woman can do, was gone.

When I moved to the UK from Chicago at 22 I was surprised that they do not do smear tests until you are 25! It was only because in the states we do smear tests at 18 that I was diagnosed and treated. I honestly feel I would have been battling cancer if I would have been left until the age of 25. Because of this I had to fight and prove my previous diagnosis to continue smear tests every six months. In my smear test results it said that I still had abnormal cells and that they wanted to do a biopsy. I was distraught. I was in a relationship with my now husband and knew that we both wanted kids. The thought of not having kids and potentially losing the man I love because of it was almost too much to handle. Despite this, God and the Universe delivered me a miracle and the nurses doing the biopsy actually decided NOT to do it as my cervix had actually regrown! I felt like I had won the lottery, I could actually carry children.

11th September 2013

It's 8am and I'm sitting in the hospital waiting room waiting to be induced as I am 13 days late. Considering my previous complications with pre-cervical cancer, I'm grateful that I can hold a baby so long, but I wanted a home birth. I was doing everything right so why is my birth plan going so wrong? I was working in London and originally planned to work up until 37 weeks. But it was an extremely hot summer and taking the train and tube everyday was becoming more draining on me, so I decided to start maternity leave at 35 weeks. I spent my days relaxing, getting everything ready for when Olivia was due to arrive on the 29th of August. I was planning a home birth so had the pool set up in my kitchen, I had everything ready for when I did go into labour. I would walk a lot to make sure I stayed active to help her come, but she didn't. The 29th came and went and I tried to stay positive; a lot of babies aren't born on time.

The midwife would come and visit me every few days to check the baby and give me a sweep. She told me to keep doing what I was doing, and Olivia would be sure to come. I walked 2 miles a day, ate spicy food, had sex, took baths with clary sage oil; I did it all. At 8 days late they had to book my induction in, just in case. I thought surely, she wouldn't be that late. My dad was due to fly in on the 12th of September, I thought Olivia would have been here already and we would have been settled into a routine, I didn't imagine that my dad would have to sit in hospital with us. I was feeling defeated. I had these amazing ideas of how I was going to cope in labour and how I would feel being the pool with soft music playing and watching my girl be born into this world, and then, in an instant my dreams fell away as I woke up on the 11th with no contractions and knowing I would have to have a hospital birth.

When we arrived at the hospital it was eerily quiet. I was in a shared ward but there was only one other woman there. I was eager to get the process underway because in my mind, Olivia would be coming that day. After an hour of monitoring me and Olivia they were able to start the induction process. They started with a 24-hour hormone strip. For most women they will allow you to go home, but not for me. When they had examined me, Olivia's head would go up, the danger being the cord getting wrapped around her neck or coming out before she does, so I had to stay in. Once the strip was in, they left me to it, I walked around a bit to try and get things started, but nothing. I was getting really distressed as I kept having different midwives and was being told different stories about the process of next steps. They also told me that my dad wasn't going to be allowed to visit or be in the delivery suite. I had no intention of him watching the birth, but I wasn't going to have him fly all the way from Chicago to sit in a hospital waiting room. All these things were not conducive to the stress free, blissful birth I had planned. Luckily, my home midwife came and sorted everything out for me. She told me exactly what the next steps were in the induction process, she even organised so my dad could stay with me up until delivery. I was feeling a bit more positive about it all until about 8pm and still nothing was happening. They told me that my partner would have to leave at 10pm and I felt devasted. I didn't want to be alone, in the states your partner can stay with you the whole time, I mean you pay for absolutely everything, but when you feel so vulnerable, you just want your safety blanket. That night my mind wouldn't shut off, I wasn't used to sleeping on my own and I just kept thinking and praying that Olivia would come.

12th September 2013

My dad arrived at the airport at 5:30am and my husband, Chris picked him up. They came to the hospital around 9:30am. At that point I had already been examined and I hadn't made much progress. At about 11am they gave me a 6-hour hormone pessary to help induce labour. I had slight contractions but nothing major. At 5pm they gave me another pessary in the hopes that this would surely work. I didn't feel any contractions and halfway into my second round of hormones the midwife wanted to examine me. Holy hell, I would not wish pain like that on my worst enemy. Not only was my cervix extremely sensitive due to all the hormones but it actually sits back towards my spine which makes my uterus tilt forward. This normally doesn't cause too many issues as in labour the cervix will be brought forward during contractions, but since I was so overdue the midwife thought it best to PULL my cervix forward. I screamed so loud that everyone on the ward could hear me, and I wasn't just screaming, I was cursing like a sailor.

On the plus side, after this happened, I started having stronger contractions, so I was hopeful. My dad and Chris left at 10pm and said they would be back in the morning if they weren't called back sooner...

13th September 2013

By morning all contractions were gone and there wasn't even a flicker of anything going to happen naturally. The ward wasn't as quiet as it was a couple days ago. All the beds were taken and as soon as someone left another came in. Shortly after Chris and my dad arrived the head midwife, Bob, and the doctor came to discuss what we were going to do next. They informed me that they would need to break my water, but first, they would need to give me an epidural. Now, when you have your heart set on a home birth so you can bring your child into the world in the most natural way possible, having your dreams shattered is a big blow. I pleaded with them to let me try gas & air first and they told me it would be better for both of us if I got the epidural. As this was my first time going into labour, I just nodded and agreed. Years later, after talking to midwives, they told me that I should have stood my ground, and that I actually have the final say, but to make things easier on them they sometimes encourage women to make a decision they don't want. But that's the problem with NHS cuts and care directed by turnover instead of patient needs, but I digress. At that I point I just wanted to meet my daughter, so I said, 'let's do it'. They asked me if I wanted to do it today or tomorrow, I was like, 'today please! I've been here for 3 days now, let's finally get the ball rolling'. They then told me that they would try to get me in today, but the ward was very busy. Every choice I wanted to make was no longer my choice and rather a decision being forced upon me.

We waited until 4pm to be told that I wouldn't be induced today, and it would have to be tomorrow. As I had been there for 3 days and the ward that was getting busier and overbooked, I asked if I could book in my induction for the next day and just have a good night sleep at home, obviously if I went into labour I would come back. As they were desperate for beds they didn't hesitate to allow me to go home, finally I had a bit of choice in my care. I later found out how booked they were when I spoke to Natalie, the only other lady that was there with me on the 11th. She was on the labour ward and got up to 7cm, so they moved her to a birthing room, her progress then slowed, and they sent her back to the labour ward! I felt so bad for her, I would have been distraught.

I went home that night and had a good meal and slept in my own bed and I knew without a doubt that tomorrow I'd finally be meeting my daughter.

14th September 2013

At a few minutes past 8am we were sat in the waiting room watching the clock tick for an hour until I was finally put into a birthing suite. They were obviously still feeling the effects of the mad rush from the night before as they had to call several off-duty midwives to assist in all the births. Goodness knows when I would have been seen if I hadn't booked in. As I settled into the birthing suite that was slightly bigger than a prison cell, I was told I would need to be monitored for an hour before they could give me an epidural. I was hoping I could have a walking epidural, but they said as I was 16 days late, I had to be monitored the whole time, which was very uncomfortable. I was finally given an epidural at about 10:30am and a half hour later they broke my water. Once they broke my water they had me bouncing on a birthing ball to help move her down. After 4 hours of nothing they examined me and decided to give me the drip. So, at 4pm I was given the drip and they started with 1ml. As I started having contractions, I noticed that the epidural wasn't working on my right side. The doctor came back in and adjusted my epidural, but it only worked for about an hour. It was the strangest feeling to be numb on my left side but feel every contraction on my right side. My contractions weren't regular enough so after 2 hours of 1ml they upped it to 2ml. The contractions became steadier and at 8pm after 12 hours of being in the hospital and 9 hours into the induction process they told me I was 4cm and by midnight they wanted me to be at 6cm. I was going crazy, why didn't my baby want to come out?! After all I've been through this week I knew it was going to be a long night. At that time, they also told me that I had a fever and that they had to give me liquid paracetamol through my canula as it worked faster than tablets.

My god does liquid paracetamol burn! It felt like my hand and arm were on fire. They slowed the medicine drip down to help reduce the burning, but it didn't stop until all the medicine was gone. They noticed that with each contraction Olivia's heartrate went down so instead of checking me again at midnight they would check me in an hour. During this time my contractions got stronger and faster, there was a lot of bloody show as well. They came to exam me at 9:30pm to find that Olivia's heartrate had returned to normal, my fever had gone and that I was 10cm! Chris and I just looked at each other and cried, we knew it was finally time. They wanted me to wait another hour before pushing to allow her head to get further down. The midwife asked me to use the toilet before I started pushing but I couldn't feel my legs to walk to the bathroom. I was then given a bed pan and tried with no success. Although, I could feel my right side, the actual sensation of needing to go wee was gone and I thought I was pushing but nothing was coming. In the end they had to put a catheter in to empty my bladder before I could start pushing.

It was 11pm, my dad had left the room as he nor I wanted him to be there whilst giving birth. I got into position and started to push, I think. Obviously, if I can't push to empty my bladder how am I going to push to get my baby out, by that time I had an epidural for 12 hours, so my left side felt like dead weight and my right side just felt like pins and needles in between contractions. As she moved down it got easier to push as I could actually feel the pressure of her being there. Chris was adamant that he was going to stay by me but ended up at the business end of things and actually really enjoyed it. After an hour of pushing my daughter, Olivia Rae Chambers was born at a healthy 8lbs 12.5oz, but the trouble was the day. The midwives had 11:59pm on their watches, but the CCG machine that I had been connected to all day said 12:01 so we were able to decide what day she was born. As I had been tethered to that damn machine for 14 hours we decided to go with 12:01am on the 15th of September, 17 days late!

Once your baby is born, you forget about the pain, you forget everything. I was enjoying my skin to skin contact when they gave me a shot in my thigh to help my uterus contract to release the rest of the afterbirth, but it was made clear that it wasn't working. After such a long induction process and labour my uterus just stopped working. They gave me a second shot to try and help but that didn't work either. They gave Olivia to Chris for some skin to skin and all of a sudden, the room was full of doctors. They had removed my epidural and were getting buckets, but why buckets? I was having a postpartum haemorrhage and my body was shutting down. I can only imagine how scared my dad must have been standing outside the door watching them bringing buckets of bloody towels out.

The bleeding eventually stopped, and I lost 1400ml of blood. I had a second-degree tear and needed four stitches as well as a catheter until I was feeling well again.

It wasn't until 2:30am that my dad was allowed back in the room, which looked like a murder scene with blood everywhere, including the walls. Between the blood loss, the hormones and the instant surge of pain from having no pain meds, I was a mess. I was shaking from the pain and crying hysterically that I couldn't hold Olivia as my arms weren't strong enough. I got her to latch to my breast but as I couldn't hold her the midwife started to express the colostrum from my breast into a syringe to give to her. They eventually gave me morphine as my body was in shock. They helped me get into a position that allowed Olivia to feed and we all fell asleep around 4am.

A few hours later at 7am I woke up and was actually feeling a lot better. I asked them to take my canula and catheter out so I could take a shower. My dad and Chris had gone back home once they knew I was okay so they could get a bit more sleep and freshen up and would be back later. I was still in the birthing suite where I breastfed Olivia again around 9am and then was moved to the post-natal ward. As soon as I was moved to the ward that feel good feeling was gone. I was on a crowded ward with other new parents who had no idea what was going on, crying babies, and no one came to see me to offer me food, water or tell me what was going on. I finally got the attention of a midwife who looked at my notes and told me that I had to stay overnight as I needed to get blood test as I lost so much blood. Why couldn't they just do the test now? I was up and walking around, not faint, so the likelihood of needing a transfusion was low. After 5 days of being told what to do, I had had enough. I demanded that I be sent home and I wanted to self-discharge. I told them I would come back the following day to get blood tests, but I wanted to be at home with my husband and my dad.

It took forever to be discharged as a doctor had to sign off on it and there was a lot of emergencies where women were being rushed into theatre. After what could only be described as the never-ending induction, at 6pm on the 15th of September I was home. The following day after my blood tests I was given iron tablets as I was considered anaemic after the haemorrhage. With the blood loss I struggled to produce enough milk and made the decision to mix feed and eventually stopped at 6 weeks. I felt defeated as I never really wanted to breastfeed but then was made to feel bad because I didn't want to do it. I couldn't win and again felt that I didn't have a choice as midwives and health visitors were saying I wasn't trying hard enough, even though I had broken and bleeding nipples, Olivia would feed for 2 hours and still be hungry. I'm in the 'fed is best' camp so when I finally felt confident enough to stick to my decision, I was a lot happier.

My dream birth couldn't have been any more different than my actual birth! We need to be more prepared for the what ifs and be flexible. I feel my birth was made all the more traumatic because I was so stuck in what I wanted that I couldn't see giving birth in any other way. Don't let anyone tell you what to do with your body! Listen to their advice and make the best decision for you. Stick to what you want as you don't want to have a negative birth or thought process about giving birth. If there is someone that is involved in your care that you do not like or trust, ask for a new one. Voice your opinion and make sure you are heard. Giving birth is an absolute miracle, your body is capable of incredible things so forgive yourself and be gentle with yourself before and after your baby. Know that every story is different, so don't let mine scare you but encourage you to know that you can have the most amazing birth, it just depends on the way you look at it. At the end of the day, my daughter was born happy and healthy and isn't that what we all want. I was affected by her birth for a long time after including the treatment I received after by heath care professionals. But after a while I realized that I am an amazing woman and mom despite what they may think by stepping into my life for 10 minutes. Remember, no one can be you, you are the best mum to your baby, and no one will ever love them the way you do. If you are struggling, ask for help, don't suffer in silence. Yes, we can do it all, but it is nice to have someone help us once in a while. If you feel like you are suffering from post-natal depression, reach out to a friend, family member or doctor. You are not alone, and it happens to 1 and 10 women, you are just as strong for getting help. I really just want you to know to not compare yourself to anyone else or my birth story to yours. I've told it to help me heal and to empower you to be a kick ass mum and to be your own advocate when it comes to your own birth story!

★★★

Michelle is originally from the suburbs of Chicago and moved to the UK in 2009. She came to get her master's degree at City University London and ended up meeting her husband just three months after moving here. When she had Olivia, they were living in Surrey and was working full time in London. After her maternity leave, she left her job and took to working nights so she could be with Olivia during the day and not rely on childcare. After falling pregnant with her second child, Henry, she knew they needed to move closer to Chris' family. They are now settled into the East Midlands and Michelle enjoys raising her kids alongside her own business. She is a Mindset Coach and Mentor specialising in vision boarding and active goal setting. By taking the Law of Attraction to the next level and utilising the power of visualisation and showing the steps to take she helps her clients achieve their ultimate dreams and desires. If you wish to connect with Michelle you can do so via her website – www.thebestyouinstruction.com

Chantal

Pregnancy. A beautiful miracle. The creation of new life. Something I had witnessed friends and family experience with ease and pure joy. And no complications to speak of. Needless to say, I was not prepared for what was to follow our initial ecstasy of a positive pregnancy result.

December 2009. Oliver and I decided it was time. We had been together eight years, bought a home together and adopted a cat called Wilson. So, for us the logical next step was to start a family. It took a few months for us to fall pregnant, but in March 2010 I grew tired, my running pace had slowed significantly, and I felt nauseous.

Cue the Clear Blue.

I waited impatiently for Oli to come home and announced it was time to test. We were both so excited and nervous. I remember I hadn't even finished peeing on the test stick and the result was clear as day – PREGNANT!!!

3 Weeks

Three weeks since my period, so very early days. We laughed and cried and hugged and for eight weeks we talked about what our baby would be like, if baby would be a boy or a girl and if he or she would look more like him or me. I couldn't wait to see him or her on screen, so those were the longest eight weeks of my life!

5 Weeks

We had kept the pregnancy quiet from everyone but my parents, who we told at five weeks. Dad, now affectionately known as Pobby, joked that we should take out insurance in case of twins. Now most people would probably heed the advice of their parents, but as Pobby is a serial joker that very few take seriously I told him, "Don't be an idiot, I'm not going to have twins."

Oh, the irony!!

12 Weeks

Seven weeks after that conversation and Oli are in the Royal Shrewsbury Hospital for the 12-week scan. Laying on the bed, tummy exposed and jelly on the belly, the dialogue with the sonographer went a little something like this…

Her: "So this is your first pregnancy. I see you are from Newtown. What brings you to Shrewsbury for your scan today?"

Me: "The Welshpool unit didn't have any appointments that fitted with my work patterns, so it was suggested I come here."

Her: "Ok. Well I'm just going to use this ultrasound machine to scan your womb for signs of a baby and listen for the heartbeat using the sonogram."

Me: "Ok."

Her: "Ok, so just sweeping around to get a location and… Here's a baby, congratulations. I'm just going to keep looking… (continues to sweep across my belly) … And here's another baby. Congratulations, you're having twins!"

Me: "I beg your pardon, was that not the same baby you just scanned?"

Her: "No, there are two babies (zooms out on the screen to show both at once) – see?"

Cue the tears. Lots and lots of tears. And the realisation that Pobby the joker was right; I should have taken out that insurance policy after all!

The first thing I did when I got out of the appointment was call my mum – "Mum, we're having twins!!"

Mum: "Yeah right, I don't believe you, stop joking with me."
Me: "It's not a joke mum, we are having twins."
Mum: [laughs] "Stop pulling my leg!"
Me: "I don't know why you're laughing, you said you would buy the pram – so make it a double."
Mum: "Oh my god, oh my god, oh my god…Robert (Pobby), Chantal's having twins!!"
Pobby: "I told you! You should've taken out that insurance!"
Me: "Thanks Dad…"

It all made sense now! The instant positive result, the intense morning sickness and tiredness from very early on. Pregnancy hormone levels are higher carrying twins.

13 Weeks

Next step… Nuchal scan. A prenatal ultrasound to check for chromosomal abnormalities and the only accurate test for a twin pregnancy. Thankfully they both came back low risk.

18 Weeks

More excitement followed at 18 weeks… The sex scan. And double the surprise again. The three possible combinations were driving me mad – boy/boy, boy/girl, girl/girl – and we wanted to be prepared with decorating the nursery, buying clothes and choosing names. I just had to know.

Right up to the day of the scan we had only agreed on girls' names. Twin 1 would be Aimee-Faye and twin 2 would be Riley Nicole. None of the boys' names seemed right for us. And we needn't have worried, because the sonographer confirmed we were having non-identical girls.

Cue the pink!

But the excitement and enjoyment of pregnancy was short-lived.

20 Weeks

At 20 weeks not only did I start to suffer with pelvic girdle pain, but my scan showed I had a grade 3 placenta previa (a condition where the placenta lies low in the uterus and partially or completely covers the cervix). I was told not to worry, that the placenta would move up from the exit as the pregnancy progressed. I wasn't, however, warned of the risks of the condition.

28 Weeks

At 28 weeks, just 3 days before my maternity leave was due to start, I woke to find I had had a bleed during the night.

Blood??!!!

I remember the sheer panic and fear and screamed for Oli to call the midwife – "Pack an overnight bag, I am sending for an ambulance to take you to Shrewsbury (35 miles away) to be checked over".

I didn't have a hospital bag packed for me or for the babies. I was only 28-weeks gone and planned to organise all this when I went on leave in 3 days' time. So, I naively packed a nighty, slippers, toothpaste, toothbrush, a hairbrush, deodorant and change of underwear, and that was it. I wasn't expecting to stay in. I thought I would be assessed as fine and sent home. It was only a minor bleed after all. How wrong was I?!

8 September 2010 – or eight nine ten as I remember it – was admission day.

The senior registrar for my case wanted to discharge me and I was all set to pack up and go at 18:00. But one of the young midwives waited until he was gone and begged me to reconsider. I was already scheduled for my 28-week scan the following day and the consultant would be doing ward rounds at 09:00. It made sense, so I stayed in.

Little did I know that would be the best decision I ever made!

9 September 2010. I saw the consultant on the ward rounds – "The bleeding is an early indicator that the twins could arrive early, so we will give you a course of steroid injections to help mature their lungs in the event that happens. You should be prepared to stay in hospital now until the babies are delivered."

*What the actual f**k did he just say? 12 weeks?! 3 months?!! In here?!!! I CAN'T!!! We haven't bought the nursery furniture, or the pram, or the clothes. We are nowhere near ready.*

Midday arrived and I received the first of the steroid injections (the next one would be coming at midnight) and proceeded to have my lunch.

Dinner time was when everything changed!

I was standing in the doorway of the dining room talking to newly made friends when I felt a trickle of fluid and what felt like a plug coming loose. I started to walk slowly towards the midwives' station, but with every step the flow got heavier until the plug went and I felt warm liquid running down my legs. I thought my waters had broken, but as I lifted my pyjama trouser leg up I saw my white DVT socks were soaked in blood.

And there was no midwife in sight.

I screamed, "SOMEBODY HELP ME!!!"

The next thing I knew, one of the auxiliary nurses had my bed wheeled right up next to me, she got me on it and ran me down the corridor to the labour and delivery ward. And out of nowhere I could hear people running behind me.

As we entered the labour room, I had one person on each arm inserting a canular; another person was taking my blood pressure; another was wheeling a foetal heart rate monitor machine up next to me and putting straps around me; another was pulling at my trousers and removing my knickers so they could use pads to monitor the blood loss; another had the ultrasound machine poised to check the babies were not visibly distressed; and yet another person was asking for a blood sample to cross match units of blood in case of surgery.

I was dazed with everyone and everything moving so quickly, yet I felt strangely calm. No one was talking to each other. They just got on with their tasks like a well-oiled machine. Then the consultant walked in and took control. As she was talking to me, I could feel my contractions starting and with each one I could feel the warmth of the blood.

A few hours into the bleeding and contractions, the Head of Neonatal came in to see me. He reassured me that, "In the event that the girls are delivered tonight, we have room for them both on the ward. At 28-weeks, there's an 80% survival rate and given you've had the steroid injections and your scans indicate they're a good size this is in their favour. They would need to be kept in a specialised incubator in which we replicate the conditions in the womb, and they would remain with us until their due date of 29 November."

80% wasn't good enough! And 12 weeks without my babies??!! Not a chance I was going to let that happen. I became blinkered and determined that they were staying right where they were. I had no idea how I would make that happen. I probably prayed, but honestly I don't remember.

After he left the room, there was a shift changeover and a new registrar was assigned to look after me. He explained that in a previous case of a twin pregnancy with placenta previa in which contractions had started, he had tried various methods to help slow and stop them and we talked through the options. I finally felt like I had some control over something that was happening to me. Together we opted for a half dose pethidine injection. Oh, my goodness, I was floating towards the ceiling on that stuff! But it worked!!

24 hours after the episode started, the contractions and the bleeding had stopped. Finally!!

29 Weeks

I had become somewhat of a celebrity on Ward 16 at RSH.

Medical students were queueing up to use me as a case study. Apparently a placenta previa in a twin pregnancy isn't an everyday occurrence.

The Head of Neonatal visited me when I returned to the ward – "I don't know how you did it, but well done! I was 99.9% certain that your babies were going to be delivered, so I was shocked when I came back on shift to find that they weren't in my incubators."

31 Weeks

29 September. My 31st birthday and I had been in hospital for 3 weeks.

I knew the breakfast, lunch and dinner menus off by heart now and was desperate to get out. Only one problem. I was supposed to be on bedrest and if I left the Ward it had to be in a wheelchair. But the doctors took pity on me and approved a "Day Release" to go for a meal with family and celebrate. I hadn't had a significant bleed in almost 3 weeks and as I wasn't far from the hospital, they were happy I could safely go out.

I had, however, started to feel unwell on my return and the following day developed a chest and lung infection with earache and tinnitus.

32 Weeks

My pregnancy bump had grown to such a weight for my small frame that I could no longer get in and out of bed without help raising my legs. And if I wanted to turn over, I had to ring the call buzzer for a nurse to help me.

Despite these struggles and the risk of bleeding, one registrar and a trainee midwife were keen to have me discharged and sent home citing the risk of hospital acquired infections from a long stay. I politely declined his invitation to leave. I did, however, invite him to bring every consultant on the Maternity Ward who had told me I needed to stay into my room for a meeting and that if each one agreed it would be a risk-free move then and only then would I leave. Funnily enough he backed down at that point.

At a later date, I read my file notes and saw that he had written up our conversation and finished by writing, "Patient refuses to go home, query domestic issues..."

If by domestic issues he meant there would be no one at home in the daytime to keep an eye on me and that my bedroom was at the top of a steep flight of stairs that I couldn't climb safely with the risk of bleeding, then yes I did have domestic issues. Idiot. I had completed a domestic abuse risk questionnaire, which was on file, and he didn't read it or ask me about its accuracy.

Senior Midwife, 'Crazy Karen', told me to ignore him and moved me to a room with its own toilet that was closer to the midwife station. She wanted to keep a close eye on me. Although I was scheduled for a C-Section on 17 November (38 weeks) she was adamant that I wouldn't last that long. And she was right.

35 Weeks + 3 days

27 October. It was 18:00.

I had been moved out of my side room and onto the main ward. No problem, the toilets were right opposite our bay, so I didn't have far to shuffle. Except there was a blockage and I had to use the ones at the far end of the ward. It was a challenge to get there and back and I required assistance getting back into bed.

Ten minutes after my bathroom visit it happened again – the bleeding and contractions were back. I rang the call bell and the midwife sent for the registrar on duty. As 'Dr Domestic Issues' came around the curtain I couldn't stop myself from blurting out, "Ah, hello. Good job I didn't go home really, isn't it?" Not sure why I felt so smug at that moment when I knew there was a good chance myself and/or the girls were at risk.

An hour later and I was back in labour and delivery, as my contractions were getting stronger and closer together and speeding up the bleeding.

28 October. 02:00 and the bleeding had stopped. Oli was about to go home when I asked him to help me turn over and get comfortable. I just got into position and the bleeding restarted. That was when it all changed. It was no longer a matter of keeping me going anymore. It was time to deliver.

I was walked to the operating theatre. As I sat on the edge of the bed, spine exposed ready to receive the epidural, the enormity of it all hit me like a freight train. I was filled with panic and fear and excitement. I would be awake for the whole thing, but I would get to hear and see my babies very soon. As I laid on the operating table, I could feel the numbness creeping up my body. It was meant to stop at my chest, but I could feel it rising to my throat. Obviously the anaesthetist knew what was happening and grabbed a bowl. I was violently sick. A very strange feeling when you have no feeling.

When the operation started, that peculiar feeling continued. Once they had cut through the layers of tissue and muscle to my womb, I can only describe the rummaging as being like someone was washing up dishes in my belly. I felt queasy and lightheaded. It was only a few days later that I was told I had been borderline for a blood transfusion.

03:49 Twin 1 (Aimee-Faye) arrived. 4lb 7oz. My heart was in my throat for the 60 seconds that followed. I hadn't heard her make a sound and there was a team of midwives standing around her. Finally, a cry! And she was brought to me. But I couldn't hold her yet.

03:51 Twin 2 (Riley) arrived. 4lb 15oz. The polar opposite to her sister, she was wide-eyed and screaming before she was even fully out.

In recovery, I got to hold them both for an hour. Then Aimee-Faye was taken to neonatal for monitoring of her breathing. It broke my heart that I wasn't able to see her for three days. The blood loss during the surgery meant I had to stay in bed, and she couldn't be brought in to me. Riley stayed with me.

31 October. Aimee-Faye was being a little minx and pulled out her feeding tube. She was brought back to me in an incubator and under a UV lamp. That was the first I knew she was jaundiced. It later turned out Riley was too, and they were both put in the incubator together. It would be another 5 days before their bilirubin levels were stable.

5 November. Bonfire Night and D Day. Two months after

first admission. We were finally all ready to go home. Lined up ready to go, it all felt so surreal.

Postnatal

I had become institutionalised and reliant on the hospital staff for our safety and well-being, advice and support. Those four walls had been my home, my safety, for so long. I didn't realise how much this would come to affect me later. I was offered postnatal counselling to help me transition, but I was so overwhelmed with everything already going on that I didn't have time to consider myself and how I felt. So, I politely declined. I wish now that I had spoken to someone.

After the C-section I felt empty. I had not gone through the natural birthing process. So even though I knew my babies were mine and I had more than earned them with the birthing trauma we had gone through, I could not bond with them.

I thought breastfeeding would help, but with my milk delayed by having a C-section and then only being able to feed Riley because Aimee-Faye was in neonatal, I was unable to produce enough to feed them both exclusively.

Cue the guilt at combination feeding.

Two months later and I came down ill over Christmas. I did not eat or drink for two days and my milk dried up almost entirely. I googled relactation, drank loads of water, took the advised supplements to support milk supply, but it was no use. It didn't work.

Cue the guilt of exclusive bottle-feeding and the feeling I had failed as a mother after only two months.

Added to that, our approach of 'divide and conquer' meant Oli and I slept separately for months on end. When the girls finally slept together in their room, I struggled moving back to our bed. I couldn't sleep for his snoring and the lack of sleep didn't do any of us any good. So, we continued to sleep separately. This I now know was the beginning of the end for our relationship.

Two years after their birth, Oli and I had split up and I was diagnosed with postnatal depression. I left Wales and returned home to Jersey.

Cue the guilt of failing as a partner too.

Neither of us had done anything wrong. We had grown apart. We had been so preoccupied with the girls and stealing time from each other that we had failed to make the time to focus on us as a couple.

I cannot and will not ever fault him as a father. For the eight weeks we were in hospital, he made the 70-mile round trip every day. Since returning to Jersey, he has seen the girls one weekend a month during term time and every school holiday for the last seven years without fail. He is an awesome dad and still my friend.

Looking back, I was incredibly hard on myself back then. I didn't take account of the fact that my family support lived across the English Channel, that we raised premature twin babies on little or no sleep for months on end. I convinced myself that 'I should be able to cope, everyone else does.' Well sorry, who exactly is this 'everyone else' and do they really always cope?

Since making twin mum friends, I have come to learn this:

It might look like other parents have their ducks in a row, but in reality, they have squirrels at a rave just like the rest of us.

It's all about the way we think about and cope with the squirrels.

But whatever you do, go easy on yourself. Make time for yourself. Don't be afraid to ask for help. And acknowledge your feelings. Don't bury them like I did.

Sometimes you won't get out of your pyjamas, or brush your hair, but you will have got through the day.

It's been nine years since the girls were born and seven years since I was diagnosed with depression. It has been a rollercoaster of emotions, but we have got through those years together. I am still in talking therapies, but we are happy and healthy. And that is what matters most.

***

Chantal lives in Jersey and is a mum to beautiful 'twin-cesses', Aimee-Faye and Riley, born in 2010. A qualified accountant, Chantal retrained in 2013 to become a massage and holistic therapist, focusing on healing trauma through the power of touch and the energies of Sekhem.

You can find out more about Chantal and get support from her and other women within her free supportive Facebook community, 'Restore Your Inner Goddess'.

http://bit.ly/JoinRestoreYourInnerGoddess

Alison

I wanted to share my birth story in hopes of inspiring and encouraging birth advocacy and childbirth education. My biggest hope is for women to make informed choices and to choose a birth plan that is in alignment with who they are and what their body and feelings are about the birthing process. Go deep within and figure out what kind of birth you want; that can be your foundation and have everyone around you knowing your birthing plan. There can be many possibilities and challenges that we can face but knowing your body, and emotional and physical boundaries are so important; and have someone to be there with you to be your advocate.

My birth story happened on October 22nd, 2015, at 4:20am. I was 34.5-weeks pregnant and all of a sudden on October 21st, in the afternoon, my waters broke. I took a shower and water was still leaking. I was wondering, "What is this?!" I had no idea. I had just moved into my new house looking to get ready for the baby to come in a few weeks. I thought I had more than enough time; My doggie, at the time, had just come home from boarding. I was looking forward to finally settling in and getting ready. I called my mom and she met me at the doctor's office; the doctor soon confirmed that my waters had indeed broken, and that the baby was coming in less than 24hrs.

I had no contractions for hours. I checked into the hospital. The doctor assured me that I was going to love the staff, and said the hospital was like a hotel, so comfortable blah blah blah, a high-profile LA hospital. I'm always a little weary of hospitals. I originally wanted a water-birth, unmedicated, all-natural, vaginal birth. My mom talked me out of it saying I should have a I should have a hospital birth in case of an emergency, but should still opt for an unmedicated, natural, vaginal birth; so, that's what I did

Weeks prior to that, my doctor who I had known for years, tried to talk me into a C-section, not knowing I would deliver super early. I was feeling pressured, but I knew I was not having an epidural or C-section. I had meditated on the baby being in the right position, down low, and I could feel the pressure down low.

I was barely 35yrs old with my first child, so it was considered high risk and especially having the baby 5.5 weeks early.

My pregnancy was so easy; no problems or stress. I probably worked too much and not relaxing pushed me over the edge. I had the normal water retention, but I felt great throughout the whole pregnancy. I had to live in a hotel during the last month of my pregnancy whilst I waited for my house to be ready. I was doing it alone, so I didn't have support. I had a business to run and had clients booked fully the day my waters broke and all the way up to my due date. So, I think those stresses contributed. They thought I maybe had GBS, a major infection, which could have caused it.

I was checking into the hospital, around 6/7pm. They knew I was coming but there were no rooms available, so they put me in a temporary room doing blood tests and talking to the doctor on staff, who I never saw again. Finally, a room became available around 10/11pm and my friends and family came to visit and stayed until 12am. Not long after they left, I was sitting in the room alone, and I started feeling a few contractions. I got hooked up to an IV and heart monitor for the baby; a belt around my waist. I couldn't move around and had to stay near the bed because of all this stuff that was hooked to me. Then, around 1am, I started feeling weird and freaking out; I felt full of panic and tried to get the nurse back in to find out if this was a normal part of the contractions or birthing process. They told me they had pumped me with a large amount of antibiotics for precaution in case I had GBS. They hadn't fully explained what they were going to do and what was being put into the IV. I'm very sensitive and any antibiotics or medication can make me feel crazy, but they didn't bother to ask me. Who knows what was pumped up into my IV; they don't tell you anything. My contractions started to get progressively worse. I couldn't get hold of any nurses; they were too busy, not too attentive. I couldn't sit due to too much pressure; I was standing the whole time. I explained to the nurse and student doctor on staff how I was feeling, and I asked how much longer the contractions would go on for. They told me I had around 24 hours in this state, that because it was my first baby, it usually takes a while before the baby comes. I have a high pain tolerance, but this was beyond painful; the contractions were back to back. In the moment, I thought if I was going to be in pain for 24 more hours, I would need an epidural, so I requested one in my pained state, but I knew I had to be farther along.

I started calling my friend and mom. My mom came back to the hospital; it took her 30-minutes to get there. Luckily, the nurse took 30-minutes to come back into the room with the epidural. Right when my mom looked at me and saw the epidural, she stopped the epidural procedure and told the nurse to check my dilation. My mom told them she thought I was in active labor and that they couldn't give me the epidural. Sure enough, they checked, and I was at 8cm at around 3am.

So, I opted out of the epidural. Shortly after, we made them check my dilation again, and I was at 10cm. My body was getting ready for labor and pushing. They still didn't want to call my doctor and prolonged my labor and pushing for around an extra 30-minutes to an hour. They were so nonchalant and kept telling me I had many more hours. I couldn't sit or lay down because of the pain. I needed to push the baby out and I couldn't wait on them.

Finally, my doctor came dancing into the room, happy and well rested, at around 4am. He said, "The show must begin!" Everything after that moment happened at the speed of light and moved fast. He told me to lay on my back, push my legs up into the air, way back into an awkward position, and told me how to breathe and push at the same time. The baby came in a few pushes, flying out, and my pain stopped immediately. It's crazy how intense the pain can be and then the pain evaporates. The student doctor delivered with my doctor. They pushed out the placenta and I had a small tear because I was early, and my baby was small. Then, I was stitched up.

I ended up having an unmedicated vaginal hospital birth; it was a good thing I was at the hospital for the NICU. I stood my ground and my mom was my advocate; I got Pitocin and didn't clot much but later learned the side effects of Pitocin. I was there for two days and didn't need much attention. I asked nurses why they were so busy, and they said everyone was opting for a C-section and they were sick from recovering from C-section throwing up, and in pain and on pain medication. I don't know if so many women really want to get a C-section or if they are bullied into it from doctors, or society, or celebrities getting C-sections and post-surgery to bounce back so fast.

I had barely held my baby and my doctor was clueless to the fact that he was having a hard time breathing. He cried but the nurse saw something and called the NICU nurses to come and get him. The scariest moment. I had no idea what was happening up there and the state he was in. I had a baby boy; 6 pounds. I couldn't go to see him for a day, and they did not prepare me with details of his condition. He was fighting for his life and it was devastating. Once he was stabilized and breathing on his own, he ended up staying in NICU for ten days, which was remarkable. I couldn't hold him for two days. I started pumping and feeding him breastmilk in feeding tubes, and then bottles, and then finally, straight from the boob. He latched on when we got home.

I believe that all that waiting down so low caused his distress. He had bruising and the cord around his neck; he needed to come out way sooner. I recovered fine, but unfortunately, my baby endured all the trauma. If I would have gotten the epidural and postponed my labor, and if my mom didn't make them check my dilation, I don't want to think about what could have happened and what other trauma would have been. They were following protocol of what usually happens and not to check dilation if waters broke so many weeks early because it could cause infection. They didn't check in with me to see how I was or ask any questions on how my body works. They acted like I was bothering them and annoying them with my questions and asking them to check in on me. They were rude at times. The NICU nurses were really great, so I am thankful for that. It's an experience I don't ever want to face again, of my baby being rushed to the NICU, fighting for his life for a few days.

My boy is almost 4.5yrs old, super strong physically and mentally, and healthy and smart, full of life; it was a success story. We are now finally stopping breastfeeding at night. He was a boob man!

I met so many moms in the NICU who delivered prematurely because of preeclampsia, and the babies had been in there for months and couldn't go home until the due date. Dedication and hope drove those mamas and their support systems. I have so much admiration for all these warrior mamas and babies.

I learned so much about how our hormones change and

the postpartum process during and post pregnancy. Our body, mind and emotions go through so much and it's so important to heal ourselves with self-care, nutrition, exercise (when the time is right), and hormone balancing. It is vital to check in with our emotions and mental health, to make sure we are optimally functioning. It's ok to ask for help if we are experiencing postpartum anxiety or depression; it's a real thing. There are so many resources, including alternative and conventional medicine. I experienced postpartum anxiety early on in my pregnancy. My anxiety went away after I got the prenatal vitamins and found out I had low progesterone; Once I took natural progesterone cream for 1-2 months, the anxiety went away while pregnant, but then it came back 3-4 months postpartum, and I acknowledged the symptoms and stopped what I was doing to be still, drink water and breathe. Sometimes I would call a friend or my mom to talk to while I was going through it. Sometimes I would get anxiety if I didn't have enough food or protein, especially because breastfeeding takes a lot out of you, burns calories and you are always starving. Once I started eating more and noticing the signs I would combat it with my favorite mantra and fight through. I went to see an energy healer very often to help heal and eventually got rid of my anxiety altogether. I always have snacks and water with me and just breathe and have a support system to call if I'm in need. After going through my journey and learning so much about pregnancy and birth and the postpartum process, I wanted to help women balance their emotions and get the right nutrition, self-care and exercise. We all heal in different ways. A wellness postpartum process is very important to implement. I help women with their emotional wellness through life coaching and use metaphysical tools to better enhance personal development and building self-confidence, self-love and positive body image. I enable transforming negative thoughts into positive thoughts to make positive change and attract all things magical.

What I know now, with all the knowledge and experience of learning and watching the whole process of childbirth and knowing the female body, is totally amazing and I am still learning whilst helping others achieve their goals in motherhood, and balancing working/mom life and healing from within.

I didn't take much maternity time, only one month, and went back to working part-time, not hiring a babysitter until after the baby was 1yrs old. I took him on client calls or brought him into my office until he was 2yrs old. I figured out the whole breastfeeding thing. My mom and brother were a big support team and babysat at night so I could work later.

I would definitely ask for more help, and now I know both sides, that we can have a birth without trauma and the ugly business side of birthing. I believe if we do research, visualize and put our intentions out there, we are prepared for anything in between. Sometimes, we just don't know what the outcome will be, but we can stand up for we want; our bodies, our choices. And, do what is necessary to be healthy and have a healthy baby.

Every birth experience is different, every baby's entrance into this world is unique, and everyone's body heals differently. Don't be hard on yourself if your body doesn't bounce back right away. It will, it takes time. Take care of yourself, your baby and your family.

I'm going to offer women's circles because I think women's support and connection is healing, and we can be on this journey together

★★★

Alison Ashley has dedicated her life to becoming a women's health and birth trauma advocate. As an IPEC certified life coach, certified health coach, hormone specialist, and an electrologist, Alison knows first-hand the trauma that can occur with childbirth. From her own personal experience and training to become a certified birth and postpartum doula, Alison deeply acknowledges that giving birth can be one of the most painful experiences in a woman's life. Through Vertical Life Purpose Coaching, Alison specializes in taking a holistic and intuitive approach to ensure clients receive long-lasting, solid and balanced results. Through this book and her coaching, Alison hopes to help the millions of women who have childbirth trauma to use holistic health and intuition to guide themselves through life with grace. Alison has been featured on TV shows including, 'This Is LA', as well as in podcasts, radio interviews and Facebook lives to speak on the topic of birth trauma as an expert in her field.

Contact Alison:
www.vlpcoaching.com
www.instagram.com/vlpcoaching
www.pinterest.com/vlpcoaching
LinkedIn – Alison Ashley
Alison is offering one-on-one coaching and group coaching and starting women's healing circles in Los Angeles. Alison offers coaching services over the phone and in person in LA.
info@vlpcoaching.com

Chelle

Where to begin?

Well, let's start with the fact I was unsure about writing this as I personally have never looked at my story as traumatic. I wasn't sure how it would fit with some of the other experiences within the book which have left lasting consequences on those involved. I was worried mine may come across as a cry for attention or like I was just wanting to be in the book for a few minutes of fame. I spent quite some time mulling things over when I concluded that this was exactly why I needed to share my births. To explain that when you are lucky enough to walk away from an event, you have the choice of how you respond. I'm not dismissing mental trauma; I'm simply sharing an alternative viewpoint in the hope of inspiring new perspective and new ways of thinking.

Yes, it obviously helped that I am trained in mindset coaching and had spent many years learning methods of self-development and coaching them, but no one is immune. I don't care how 'strong' or 'capable' or 'successful' someone is, there is always the possibility that the dark clouds will descend when circumstances combine to create the perfect storm.

And my storm was brewing! But more on that soon.

As I tell my story you can expect it to be brutally honest and a little funny, with a few F-bombs for good measure; if you are offended by swearing then I apologise in advance and no hard feelings if you skip past it.

So... lets go back to where it all began so you can understand what comes later.

In 2004 I was diagnosed with polycystic ovarian syndrome and given less than a 1% chance of naturally conceiving, and if by some miracle that happened, there was less than a 5% chance of giving birth to a healthy baby. Now, at 18-years-old, this wasn't an issue; I had no thoughts of children at that time and was happy doing my thing and living my life. I was always out partying, buying nice clothes, spending a fortune on makeup and my hair, and all the things most 18-years-olds do. I actually thought I was ok with the thought of no children. Well that's what I told myself.

Fast forward to early 2011 and suddenly the thought of a family arrived. Knowing what I knew, it was a case of praying for a miracle and boy did I pray! Each month it didn't happen my heart sunk, and as the months went on, it felt like it was never going to happen. It's funny how we know the odds are stacked against us but that still didn't stop the self-blame and criticism. I was beginning to feel like a failure!

In October 2011, two little lines turned pink. I couldn't fucking believe it and the following 9 months I was a bag of nerves wondering about the endless ways that things could go wrong. On the outside I seemed perfectly calm and relaxed, but my mind would race.

On June 4th, 2012, my princess arrived into the world after a mammoth 46 hours. I missed summer night proms with Russell Watson and a jubilee street party. But she was worth it! I was over the moon and so grateful to have a healthy little princess in my arms that the pain just melted away and was like it hadn't existed.

I had wanted a water-birth but that wasn't possible as during labour I had low movements from baby, so I was strapped to the monitors throughout. But my plan for just gas and air was successful, despite a little wobble about 44 hours in when I was exhausted and just plain fed up of being stuck on a bed.

My partner had always said he didn't want to see what was going on when it came down to the nitty gritty, but the universe had other plans and this part is too funny not to share...

Every few hours he was nipping out to update the families (and the guests at the street party) with how things were going. "Will it be ok to just nip out and tell them what's going on?" he said, and the midwife laughed and replied, "Of course, take your time! At this rate we have a good few hours left."

A short while later I got the urge to push and shouted to the midwife, "She is coming". The midwife smiled and said, "No, she isn't." "SHE IS COMING NOW!!!!!" As the midwife turned to look, her face dropped, "OH SHIT! She is! Someone find dad NOW!!!" As she raced to put her gloves on and get ready she was saying, "Don't push yet, let's wait for him", but my body had other plans and took control just as, you guessed it, Dad walked through the door facing the business end! Oops!!!

Just 6 months later I started feeling familiar signs, but I couldn't be, surely not! I was on the pill and I wasn't lucky enough for a second miracle, was I?

The months flew by and on the 20-week scan we found out we were having a boy (he was proudly displaying his crown jewels on the scan). This time I hadn't been so anxious, but it was always there in the back of my mind, the million and one disastrous scenarios waiting to fill my consciousness without warning.

Again, I went past my due date, but this time we had to evict my little man as he was not budging. I thought that was a sign he would be a lazy, sleepy little boy, but I got that wrong!

Despite having contractions, the hospital weren't happy with the frequency and strength of them, so I was put on the hormone drip – oh my fucking god, that's the work of the devil! From the minute it began to work I had no break in contractions. One would end and within a breath the next stated. Even moving or having my bump touched would trigger another. But it worked, it was moving things along and before I knew it I felt that urge again. I had warned the midwife about the rapid arrival of Eva, so she was gloved up and ready. And just like before, without even a push, my beautiful baby boy took his first breaths.

In the summer of 2015 we moved home, Eva was about to start nursery in the September, and we thought now would be a good time to try for a third. We knew it might not happen but this time it was more a case of 'if it happens, it happens'.

Two and a half years passed, and I began looking forward to Alfie starting full time school and planned my working days knowing I could have my evenings back.

Then … Miracle number 3!

At the 12-week scan we found out I was actually nearly 16-weeks along, so we only had four weeks to wait until we found out if we were team blue or pink. Little did I know that my world was about to be turned upside down and thrown around in the meantime.

One Friday started as an ordinary day, nothing special apart from the kids had finished for half term and we only had a few days until the 20-week scan, but by 4pm it felt like the ground had opened up beneath my feet as I heard the words, "Can you show me how to use the washing machine until I leave please?" And just like that I was a pregnant single mum.

Eva and Alfie are switched on and aware so I did everything I could to hold it together in front of them, I would cry in the kitchen as I made tea or washed the dishes, cry in the shower and for the first few nights, I cried myself to sleep. I was an emotional wreck.

I was angry, rejected, sad, betrayed, furious… I was every negative emotion there is and the hormones didn't help.

I remember going to the scan and the kids were coming with us as they were really excited. Eva wanted a girl and Alfie wanted a boy; one of them would be leaving happy and the other would not be impressed. The sonographer gleefully asked, "So, is this the last, or will you be having another?" It took every fibre of my body to hold it together and not break down or go off on a hormonal rant. Afterall, she had no idea what was going on.

About a week or so later, the dark and angry clouds began to lift a little and I had times where it was like nothing was going on, and then without warning, it was like I was walking round in a personal thunderstorm.

I knew I needed to shift my mindset, and quickly, before I got lost in a never-ending fog. I got back to what I had learned over the years with the purpose of protecting my mental health. I was living the perfect storm for pre and post-natal depression and I desperately wanting to do anything in my power to avoid that.

As we got to about week four, I was offered the opportunity to be a co-author in a book about mums in business, and without even knowing how I would fit it in, I said yes! It was the perfect distraction and task to focus on while achieving a lifelong ambition of being a published author. I also knew if I could do that while I had so much going on, it would be the proof I needed to give myself that nothing could break me, that there was nothing I couldn't achieve and no challenge too big for me to overcome.

By the time I got to the 7-month mark, I was mentally the strongest I had ever been; life was great, and business was booming.

At 36-weeks, at the sizing scan, they detected high cord flow, which was not really explained well but I researched it and found that it was the equivalent of the baby having high blood pressure. They wanted me back a week later for a follow up and to make plans from there. A week later, there was still high cord flow and I was sent home with strict instructions that the minute I had reduced movements or felt anything wasn't right, I had to go straight for assessment.

We got to week 38 and my little prince hadn't been his usual active self in the morning, so by the afternoon, I was calling the assessment unit and had to go in for monitoring. Typically, the monkey started moving about as soon as the monitors were put on, but the scan revealed I still had high cord flow and the decision was 50/50 to leave me or induce me. They asked my thoughts, and something told me that it was time. It felt like the right thing to do, so I said we would go for being induced and I was taken round to the ward.

Contractions started immediately and I was thinking 'wooo hoooo!' But after an hour they stopped, and I just knew this wasn't going to be a walk in the park as I had hoped. Again, my water-birth dreams were poo-poo'd and I spent the majority of Tuesday strapped to the monitors and restricted to my bed. Any opportunity to get up and walk around was a blessing, I'm not the sit still type, and I was going a little cray cray, especially when my internet signal would drop.

You see, the book that helped me keep my sanity and gave me focus was due for release in just two days and I was loving the hype and excitement the authors were sharing together, as well as the marketing push.

My girls from the book and my entire following were constantly waiting on birth updates. I had a whole army sending push vibes and he still wasn't having any of it.

Then came the conversation on the Wednesday morning, "We can either send you home and see if you go naturally over the next few days or try to break your waters, but it may be difficult."

I was going nowhere; I knew I needed to be there, and I also knew that my little man wanted to share his birthday with the book. I joked with the other authors about it and half an hour later I got a message to say the book was live! Holy fucking shit, I was a published author marketing my book from the maternity ward and determined to have the #1 best-seller badge before I went to the delivery rooms.

And just like that we had the number 1 badge, my waters were broken, and the contractions were starting but that was all too simple for me and I knew I was in for a bumpy ride.

After an hour or so the midwife said they weren't happy with the strength of the contractions and if they didn't improve within two hours they would be putting me on the hormone drip. I physically shuddered at the thought and began visualising a drip free birth. It was around the hour mark and they said they had decided to start the drip now as there had been no improvements at all so waiting another hour was unlikely to have any major effects.

"Right Chelle, here we go! We got this! We are tough stuff!", my inner voice said to me.

And just like last time, within 15-minutes of the drip going in, I was getting constant contractions and the intensity of the pain was becoming that intense, it was taking my breath away. All I was breathing was gas and air as it was, that mouthpiece never left my mouth.

Suddenly, they were concerned that the baby's heartbeat wasn't picking back up after the contractions (I'm not surprised as there was barely a break between them) and his movements were too far apart for their liking (again, it's hard to move in a continually contracting space).

At this point panic quickly set in, "I can't cope, what if something happens? Why can't things just be easy? Have I not been through enough? I can't take this, I've had enough, I'm exhausted, what if things get worse?" Thoughts raced through my mind and the pain this time literally stopped me from breathing properly.

I had a blunt midwife demanding I calm down as they couldn't monitor the heart rate if I kept moving, and if I didn't sort myself out immediately, she would need to put the internal heart monitor on his head. It felt like before she had even taken a breath after speaking, her hand was up there attaching the wire. Again, she told me to calm down immediately.

I was about to fucking snap and she was, unfortunately, going to be on the receiving end. As if by magic and within three seconds, I knew everything was going to be perfect, that I had this, that I was more than capable, I wasn't alone.

"There was a time, I used to look into my father's eyes..."

"TURN THE RADIO UP!" I demanded; This was the song that always came on when I needed it the most. It was a song me and my dad had loved and had to be listened to loudly. My breathing instantly calmed, and I felt this unbelievable strength take over.

"No, we need it quiet."

"TURN THE FUCKING RADIO UP NOWWWW!!!!!" I roared, I was not taking no for an answer; the radio was going to be turned up by my ex, the midwife or I would fucking do it myself (somehow).

I took a deep breath, I centred myself, I remembered my training that moments before had completely left my brain.

I HAD THIS!

It was around 9.40 and I looked at my ex and said baby will be here by 10:10, I originally said 1am.

The midwife said you cannot push whatsoever, you are barely even 5cm dilated, you will shatter your pelvis and tear yourself in two just trying.

"OH, COME ON YOU GOT TO BE FUCKING KIDDING ME??? I feel the urge to push now!"

The midwife explained that when my waters had been broken the whole lot had been drained so baby's head was sat on my cervix and baring down, but I was nowhere near ready.

"DO NOT PUSH, YOU NEED TO FIGHT IT!" came the instruction.

Now, for anyone reading who has never experienced fighting the urge to push a baby out, I can only liken it to fighting the urge to have a poo when there is no toilet nearby. You know, when you have to concentrate so fricking hard NOT to do what your body is telling you and trying to do! It's like tug of war: the body vs the mind.

I took another deep breath, closed my eyes and went into a bubble. I was fully aware of what was going on, but my mind needed to be fully focused on fighting the urge to push, of coping with the immense pain knowing that my little boy wasn't happy in there.

Fifteen minutes later, I heard the midwife say, "You need stronger pain relief. I'm getting you some now." Now, during this time I had been in a trance, not uttered a word, not moved, not complained. Without even opening my eyes or removing the gas and air pipe, I point blank refused. "You are not giving me a drug that may effect his heart rate just to reduce my pain, I am fine as I am."

I could see her eye roll with my eyes shut.

"Don't underestimate me!" I barked.

The room was becoming noisier and noisier by the minute, people coming and going, hushed conversations round the monitors, phone calls being made and then the NICU bed in the room was set up.

Suddenly, my crystal bracelets were being taken off my wrist and a second IV line was being fitted. It all felt rushed, panicked, urgent.

I opened my eyes and asked, "What's going on?" No one

had bothered to even speak to me or the baby's dad.

"We are prepping theatre and taking you down for emergency c section as the baby is struggling and you are severely dehydrated, so we need to pump you full of fluids and stop the drip first." I was later told they put two litres into me in a matter of minutes but I'm not sure if that was an exaggeration or even possible, and that they don't normally just stop the hormone drip abruptly but instead lower the dose bit by bit. So, this was a pretty fucking important call they made.

My badass inner voice was loud and clear, "We need a pow wow now! We got this, cracked pelvis, torn insides and anything else will heal, follow your intuition, trust your body, anything is better than not being the first person to hold him! I got..."

Before I had even finished my internal pep talk and with no warning, a hand was suddenly inserted into me, and just like that, my control was broken.

"Get your hand out if you don't want me to push!"

"I need to see how far you are", as she shook her head looking at the midwife hovering at my side.

"Get your hand outttt!"

Too late! As she removed her hand, my body took over. "He is coming now!!!!" And out he came, no pushing, I simply just stopped fighting myself.

Harry was placed on to my chest as the packed room began to empty, showing us that his lungs were fine. He lifted his tiny head right up and looked me dead in the eye with a look of, 'Sorry about that Mum, but thanks!'

His heart rate was perfect, he was perfect!

Turned out, the midwife hovering at my side was about to give me an injection to stop the labour, and the breaks were about to come off my bed as the situation had become almost critical.

Then came the internal exam. I hadn't dare move in the few

minutes since, in case I had done some major damage to my pelvis. I almost didn't want to know. But just like everything, life had already thrown at me I knew I would figure it all out.

Gas and air at the ready, I gave the nod to do her thing. She had the most puzzled look on her face. "I don't know how but you are absolutely fine, you haven't even got a graze, let alone any tears, you were only just 8cm. Clearly, I did underestimate you!" Told you so, I thought, but I was too happy to say. "You can go for a shower and the toilet when you are ready", the midwife said, as she was finishing up.

Now, as any woman who has given birth naturally and had grazes/tears will tell you, that first wee fucking stings worse than the whole labour. It's quite literally the definition of water torture. I hesitantly sat on the toilet and anticipated the all too familiar razor blade sting… but it wasn't there! My most chaotic birth of the three and I walked aware fully intact… the irony was not lost on me.

Within an hour of giving birth, I had showered and been moved to the ward for an overnight stay. Once the baby's Dad had come back from calling his girlfriend, I grabbed my dressing gown, my phone and said, "Back in 10." I was off for a walk to celebrate the fact I still could, and to let all my online birthing partners know that Baby Harry had made quite an entrance into the world and shared a birthday with the book, just like I knew he would.

So, why don't I see that as traumatic? Well, to be totally honest, right from the moment it was over, I knew how unbelievably lucky I was and that while the birth may have been far from smooth sailing, the outcome was totally perfect. And I was going to choose to focus on the outcome and nothing else.

I guess it was also part of my plan for starting my new journey with a healthy mindset. I knew dwelling on the what ifs would only breed more negative thoughts. I still had many challenges to come over the following days, weeks, months and years, and I needed to pick my battles wisely.

The day to day practicalities of being a single mum with a newborn were actually quite easy. Looking back, I can honestly say I was much happier, calmer and balanced third time round than I was with Eva or Alfie. I had been through a crazy evening where my physical and mental willpower had been tested to the extreme, so I knew motherhood couldn't throw anything at me that I couldn't handle without missing a step.

I suppose you could say I'm that annoying type that is up and out like nothing had happened, and that's totally true; I did the school run on the Friday morning, met by the most shocked faces, and was doing the food shop on the Saturday.

But that's just me! That's the way I am wired. And I don't think that will ever change. Yes, I do have bad days, I am actually human despite what some might say. I allow myself to feel the emotions coming up, I explore them, I learn, I heal, I seek the solutions and the positives, and I move forward.

It's being wired like this that I credit as saving me from pre or postnatal depression, because I can honestly say I don't know how I would have come back from that, that would have been only one of two things in this world to actually break me. And somehow I avoided both!

To those reading who have beaten or are currently fighting PND, you have my complete and utmost respect for being courageous and strong beyond comprehension.

To those reading who didn't get to experience life with their bundle of joy, my heart breaks for you.

To those reading who are the partners or a support system for anyone above, know that you are remarkable people with hearts of gold. The world needs more like you.

★★★

Chelle Clarke is a single mum of three, multiple best-selling author, and transformation queen for female entrepreneurs. Chelle has a mission to guide women to unlock their ideas of success through combining strategy, mindset and spirituality. Chelle is the UK Head Ambassador for Child Author Project, creating young published authors and raising awareness of mental health issues.

In 2020, Chelle committed to reaching and working with 10,000 women through her existing and upcoming programmes, courses and new hybrid transformation sessions. Chelle is also an intuitive card reader, crystal practitioner and energy healer.

You can get in touch via Chelle's website or Facebook:

www.soulvibration.co.uk

www.facebook.com/soulvibrationuk

Sarah

There's absolutely nothing like the feeling that you have when you first hold your child. For me, everything else that had happened to me melted away for a couple of minutes.

In December 2014, I was very shocked and absolutely delighted to find out that after being infertile, after seeing the infertility clinic for a year, and after I had given up hope, I was pregnant. The day I found out I had already been booked in for a scan. The hospital thought I might have a complication after my latest procedure as I had been quite unwell, but now I knew why.

A few weeks later, my third scan revealed I was carrying twins! Shock hit me, I was petrified, how on earth could I breastfeed two babies at once? But that soon turned to absolute joy.

I have never formally been diagnosed with PTSD, as I was in denial at the time, but over the course of writing this story, it has become clear to me that perhaps I am suffering with this. My story is one of heartbreak and grief, but also one of strength and positivity. To go from your world falling apart right in front of you, to actually feeling happy again is a long road, a bumpy one, but achievable. Grief never leaves you but the way you live your life around it is something you're in control of.

The first sign of anything wrong with my pregnancy was at 11-weeks. I had started spotting and had a private scan booked in, as I wanted to see the twins again. After the scan, I was still spotting and something felt wrong, so my sister and I made our way to A&E. I was taken to a trolley surrounded by other people who were poorly, and inside I knew what was going to happen, I didn't want them to be there when it did. After about half an hour, the trolley was overflowing with blood. I was panicking, my sister ran to get anyone she could find. Suddenly, all the other cubicles fell silent, they knew by then that I was pregnant and something bad was happening.

My jeans were cut off me and I could tell by the doctor's face that I had lost my babies, but the nurse was insistent that I hadn't miscarried. I held onto her hope for dear life, but I had to wait about ninety minutes before I was scanned.

Ninety minutes later the babies were on screen, fine and both waving at me! I was told a clot had burst and that was the reason I bled so much. I spent the next few weeks feeling cautious, came off working ward rounds at hospital and stayed in the clinic, but still, I just didn't feel right. I was told it was just the twin pregnancy, it was extra weight which would make me feel more tired.

Skip to 22-weeks…

My waters broke one morning, and after examination at hospital I was told I would have to stay in until the twins were born. There was a very low chance of survival if I went into labour and had to sign some forms to say that if they came early and they were alive, just to give them pain relief. At 24-weeks, I changed it so that they would receive life support, and at 26-weeks, I was delighted when I could finally use the monitoring machine twice a day. I celebrated with the other girls in my ward by ordering in a takeaway. Those girls kept me sane, they were also all in for PPROM – Preterm Premature Rupture of the Membranes.

At 26-weeks, I really started to feel even more anxious, something really wasn't right. Green baby poo had started appearing when I wiped, but I was dismissed and told, "It's ok, it's just a little bit." My fears and worries were completely being ignored. At 27-weeks, I started bleeding a little, but again, I was told I was fine, I started having what I describe as back labour, but again was dismissed.

One afternoon at 27-weeks and 4 days, I begged the consultant and registrar to scan me; I was still bleeding, had poo coming out and I didn't feel well. They wouldn't scan me and assured me that if they thought anything was wrong they would intervene. Three hours later, all hell broke loose when I went to the bathroom. I stood in a huge puddle of blood, with more still pooling around me. The other pregnant ladies started shouting for help and pressed the buzzer, and a few minutes later, a midwife strolled in, she took one look at me and told me to stay put! She returned a few minutes later with a wheelchair and said she couldn't get hold of the doctor, so was wheeling me round herself to the delivery suite.

I spent from the Tuesday evening right through to Friday afternoon in the delivery suite. The same consultant who had earlier told me I was ok was still adamant I was ok. As the monitoring of my babies showed they were fine, no one listened to me; I was just the vessel to carry babies and my thoughts didn't matter, at all.

On the Friday morning, a new consultant came in and examined me. He decided that I was losing too much blood, my placenta had ruptured three days earlier and that I need an emergency c section; finally, someone had listened to me and made the decision that my babies were actually in distress.

At 3.01pm, my son Teddy, twin 1, who's waters had broken at 22-weeks was born weighing 2lbs 12oz, followed by Tilly, twin 2, at 3.03pm weighing 2lbs 5oz. I met Tilly briefly when they whisked her off to intensive care, I didn't see Teddy as they had already taken him.

Three hours later, my son Teddy passed away on my chest, as I squeezed breast milk onto his lips, the moment captured on camera by my sister. He had lost too much blood. It wasn't a hard decision to make when I told them to turn the machine off, it was the right thing as he had been resuscitated nine times by then, had had two blood transfusions and they had tried different life saving equipment, but he was deteriorating very quickly.

Tilly, the smallest of the two spent nine weeks in Neonatal Intensive care. She had a couple of blood transfusions, had a hole in her heart, was diagnosed with chronic lung disease and had me very worried a lot of times. Not being able to stay in the same building as her overnight was heart wrenching, especially as my son had just passed away. Each day, I had to travel forty minutes home, to repeat the journey again the next day. I was consumed by grief, but also joy, those two massive emotions together are indescribable, but you can only imagine how it felt.

Tilly came home at 9.5-weeks-old; she was only 4lbs, tiny and had to have her breastmilk topped up with a fortifier. The midwife kept insisting I needed to give her more bottles with fortifier as my milk wasn't fat enough! And I was even told that I was negligent if I didn't do so, so at 13-weeks old, I gave up breastfeeding as I felt pushed into a corner and didn't want my daughter to die like her brother. In hindsight, the midwife was wrong for what she did, she set in motion for me a rollercoaster of fear for the next two years that my daughter would die!

Tilly got ill very often, because her lungs were weak and because she was premature. Each day, I expected her to die; I felt like I had to make the most of every moment with her as it wouldn't last.

I would wake up so happy to see her smile, see her older brother cuddle her, then be drawn back to the feeling that today could be our last day with her. I feared her catching the slightest of colds, whenever she would end up back in hospital for her lungs and breathing, I felt like I would have to let her go, like I did with her brother.

It was a cruel feeling I was having every day, and a feeling that lasted for two years, not one day going by when I didn't think she might die. I was also grieving for her twin brother Teddy and looking after the complex needs of my eldest son, who had lost his vision during my pregnancy, but somehow I gathered hope from somewhere, I have no idea where, but I had hope and fear running through my mind each day.

When Tilly was two-years-old, she had an operation. Seeing her go to sleep and then being taken into theatre was the most difficult thing I had gone through since turning her brothers machine off. I was sick, I cried, sick some more and prayed to Teddy to help save her life, like he had before. She finally came around and was very much alive. We had a lot of ups and downs for a few weeks, but that was the turning point for me when I no longer thought every day that she would die. Her airways had been permanently unblocked, she could breathe properly, she could breathe at night and I could finally start to relax and enjoy being a mum. Although I don't have this daily feeling anymore, I do still worry whenever she is ill that something might happen, but I don't dwell on it too much and I don't make myself sick with worry.

Periods are a normal part of every woman's life. I started mine when I was fourteen; They've always been on the heavier side and painful, but I just got on with it, like we do. I'm now age 42 and periods play a huge part in PTSD for me.

For the first year after Tilly and Teddy had been born my periods hadn't bothered me too much, I suppose I had a lot of other worrying to do, like worrying my daughter would die, but the day before Tilly's 1st birthday I started the most horrendous period ever! I already was distraught by the 1-year anniversary and birthday and was mentally in turmoil. How was I supposed to celebrate my daughters 1st birthday and be happy when on the same day one year earlier, my son had been born alive and then had died?! The period gave me flashbacks of me standing in that bathroom a year earlier, bleeding all over the floor, the pain was intense, and I was being reminded of what I had suffered, it was horrendous! From that point, each month when I had my period, I would have flashbacks, I would sweat, feel sick, panic, and want to curl up in a ball and disappear; it was just so unfair to have this reminder every month of what I went through.

On the 2nd anniversary and Tilly's 2nd birthday, I came on my period the day before AGAIN! What the hell?! Why was I being tortured so much? Was I to expect this at the same time every year, as a reminder of what I went through, as if I had forgotten and needed reminding?

Four years on and those monthly periods send me back to that bathroom, that Tuesday at 7pm, that Tuesday when the consultant told me I was fine, that Tuesday when three other heavily pregnant ladies saw me standing in a pool of my own blood, the blood that meant my children were in danger, the blood that led to my son's death. I hate periods so so much because of the memories they bring back, but who am I to know what's right for my body?! I asked for a hysterectomy and was told I was too young! At age 41! And after all I had been through, I feel like I should be in charge for a change, and I should be able to make that decision, but again a doctor knows better than I do.

I still hate periods, they are a trigger for me, and only recently I thought that I should really seek help for PTSD, so that is my next step.

Life has been hard the last 4.5 years; grief doesn't just disappear. For me, it's still there, but I have learned to deal with my grief in positive ways. If my son's waters that had broken at

22-weeks had caused me to go into labour, then neither of my babies would be here, but he hung on until 28-weeks to save his sister, to give her a fighting chance at life. I look at my daughter and know that a huge part of her brother is in her, and that helps me get through the difficult times.

Nearly five years on from all of that, my life has changed so much. I am self-employed and have a business that helps children with Special Educational Needs and Disabilities, and their parents too. I have become a number one bestselling author by sharing my story with others, and helped them to realise that it's ok to have the feeling we have when we lose a child, and I've helped people to know it's ok to talk about their child, to keep their memory alive.

Grief never leaves us, but it doesn't have to define how we live the rest of our lives. I never thought I would be happy ever again, but our little family is very happy. I can laugh and smile, I can talk about my son and not feel that I need to keep quiet.

***

Dedicated with love, to Teddy Auger.

***

Sarah is a mum of three; she only has two of these beautiful children of hers to look after. After the death of her son in 2015, life was at a standstill, but almost five years on, her life is full speed ahead, and she is happy once again.

Sarah started her business, The Sensory Fairy, in 2017 to help children and parents find sensory clothing and resources for special education needs and shares her experiences of SEN to help others.

Already a number one best-selling author, Sarah believes that talking about and sharing the moments in our lives that have caused us the most pain can not only be a lifeline for others facing the same struggles, but is also a great part of healing for ourselves too.

You can find Sarah over at:

www.thesensoryfairy.co.uk

www.facebook.com/thesensoryfairy

www.instagram.com/thesensoryfairy

David

Dad's Perspective

"He hasn't gone. He is with me constantly"

I was 21 years old when one of the saddest and most challenging experiences of my life occurred. In the years that have followed, it's a subject that I've rarely talked about – only to a select few of my most trusted friends and in my rare and vulnerable moments.

When a request came through for me to share this baby trauma experience within a chapter in this book, I contemplated whether or not I had the strength to retrace and write about such a traumatic experience.

I concluded that it might help people who find themselves going through a similar experience.

And so, here is my story. I share it with love and empathy.

31 years ago

This all happened what feels like a lifetime ago. In fact, sometimes, it feels like I'm reflecting on a different life to that of my own. It's actually like I'm looking back on the memories of another person. Interestingly, I hear many people who have suffered from similar trauma referring to this type of detachment – of feeling like they are reflecting on a film about someone else's life.

The story commences in 1988. After a day at work, I was heading home to my rented flat in Derbyshire. As I walked through the old-fashioned cobbled back yard, the one that paved the way to my flat, I glanced through the window of my neighbour's apartment. Debs was my friendly and sociable neighbour and there she was, stood at her kitchen window. On this day, instead of her usual big smile, Debs had an unusual serious look on her face. She tapped on the window and beckoned me in with a curl of her finger.

The crumpled piece of paper held a secret

As I stepped through the front door, I noticed that my beautiful girlfriend, Julie, was sat at the kitchen table. Julie had tears in her pretty and striking blue/green eyes. I noticed she was clutching a small piece of paper in her hand. I became anxious at the uncertainty of the situation and so I quickly questioned;

"What's going on? What's wrong?"

Julie looked up and tried to avoid making eye contact with me, as she gingerly passed me the piece of paper. I unfolded the white square shaped note and studied what was written on it.

It took me a time to focus. It was a pregnancy test result and there was a tick to indicate a positive result.

As I look back and try and summon back the memories and the emotions from that moment and day, I now realise that, as a naive and inexperienced 21 year old, I didn't have the maturity or the life experience to take in what this news really meant for us.

A feeling of pride and excitement

Back then, my immediate reaction was one of pride and pleasure. Even though myself and Julie were very young and had endured a short and topsy turvy relationship, at the time, we were happy, or at least that is how I remember it. I was going to be a dad and the prospect excited me.

I smiled at Julie and said, "Wow, this is great news."

She stood up and gave me a firm hug. I could feel her body trembling with nervousness and her tears were rolling down my exposed neck.

"I wasn't sure how you were going to react" she sobbed.

My neighbour Debs beamed at me over Julie's shoulder.

"I told her you'd be thrilled" she said, as she stepped in for a group hug.

"You two will be make a great mummy and daddy."

After a warm cup of tea and several moments of acclimatising to the news and sharing several of those exchanged glances that break into smiles, Julie and I left Deb's flat and navigated the few steps back to our own home.

Nestled on our beige, floral draylon sofa, we sat and talked for a few hours. We held hands and I gave Julie the reassurances that I sensed she was looking for. Julie knew that I loved kids.

It was time to become a man

I remember feeling a surge of motivation and mentally concluding, right there and then, that I needed to get a better job, I needed to grow up, I needed to become a man and I needed to provide for my young family.

In the weeks that followed, I remember attending our

first 12-week baby scan. We were both present with a mix of nervousness and excitement. I should not have worried. The baby's heartbeat was prominent.

"All appears just as it should" came the reassuring words of the smiling nurse.

For the next several weeks, all of the talk in our flat was about babies – cots, pushchairs, whether we wanted a boy or a girl and if our flat was suitable to bring up a baby.

Julie's parents went from a reaction of being totally appalled at the news to slow acceptance. As the weeks passed, I felt their coolness towards me lifting. Julie's mum commenced knitting baby cardigans and bonnets and her dad talked to me about our need to get a proper house, instead of the drafty rented flat that was our home at the time.

The start of the nightmare

My work prevented me from attending the next 20-week scan. I recall coming home from work and being welcomed by Julie and her mum. Julie's eyes were red with tears and she looked tired. My heart sank with dread. I knew something was seriously wrong.

Julie began to tell me what had happened. The scan had picked up an issue. The baby, which we learned was a little boy, had a condition called gastroschisis.

Gastroschisis is a birth defect of the abdominal (belly) wall. The baby's intestines form outside of the baby's body, exiting through a hole beside the belly button. The hole can be small or large and sometimes other organs, such as the stomach and liver, can also be found outside of the baby's body.

Looking for reasons to be positive

Back in 1988 there was no Internet to use for us to conduct our own research. Nowadays, it's easy to check Google and see this condition only affects 1,871 babies per year in the USA.

We were desperately anxious and the only information we had access to was provided by the doctors who, despite the desperately worrying description of the condition, assured us that the baby could be put through a small operation to rectify the issue. They gave us hope.

We were given a positive example of this and actually met the parents and a child who had emerged from a similar challenge in Sheffield. Despite our inevitable fears, this was more than enough to give us the determination to proceed with the pregnancy. Naturally, the other options were discussed, but a termination of the pregnancy was far away from our thoughts.

In the months that followed, we tried our best to remain positive. Julie had a few of the usual issues during the pregnancy and the condition suited her. As many people would say about a pregnant lady, at times she looked totally radiant. Like most expectant parents, we both enjoyed feeling the baby movements at bedtime or when watching television on the sofa.

Beautiful Brady

Very early into January 1989, Julie started to feel unwell and a little strange. This culminated in the onset of early contractions. At just 28 weeks, we were very worried. It was the early hours of the morning when an ambulance came to get us, and we were transported to the hospital. I remember doing my best to remain calm and reassuring, but I had a sick feeling that almost took over me. I had no control over what was about to happen, and I felt helpless.

As they lay Julie down on the hospital bed and strapped on various monitors, I could tell by the look on the doctors and nurses faces that they were anxious. Julie was in serious pain, crying out loud and one of the nurses asked me to leave the room to sit outside.

"It's best you are not here for the next part but Julie will be ok with us" were the encouraging words from the nurse.

I have no solid memories of how long I was sat in the busy hospital corridor but it felt like at least an hour. My most vivid memory is hearing a baby cry.

The next thing I remember is a plastic incubator being wheeled out. I stood to take a look and my heart melted. There lay the tiny, wriggling frame of my first son, Brady.

I cried instantly. It was an uncontrollable surge – the feeling of such powerful love that I had never experienced before and one of total helplessness. I so wanted to help Brady, but I had no power other than that of prayer and hope.

At 28 weeks pregnancy term, Brady was just 2 pounds and 10 ounces. His little tummy area was wrapped in surgical plastic and the nurse explained that he needed to go for checks and almost certain immediate surgery.

I was in an emotional spin. Julie had needed to be severely cut to ensure Brady could be eased out with no damage to his tummy. She looked tired, pale and totally drained. I remember giving her a hug and not having any suitable words to offer. All I could say was that he was beautiful and that I was sure he would be ok. We both knew how delicate the situation was and that his young life was so fragile and under threat.

The surgery

Brady immediately went through several hours of surgery. It was the one of the longest waits of my life. The surgeon, a doctor named Mcallan, looked totally exhausted when he came out of the Operating Theatre to see me.

The doctor explained our baby's condition and the procedure he had just completed. It was not good news. Brady's tummy had trapped tightly and cut off the blood supply to the intestine on the outside of his stomach wall. The surgery removed the dead tissue and sought to lengthen some of the intestine that was left. This should grow and serve to ensure that Brady could absorb food in years to come.

The operation had gone as well as it could but there were major infection risks with such a tiny and premature baby. I was in a daze and my emotion was just a mix of hope and desperation. I did not know how to be – what to say, what to do or where to go. I could not make sense of anything. I was disorientated.

Julie needed some time in hospital and then bed rest at home in order to recover from the deep cuts that had been administered to get Brady safely out of her tummy and without damaging his tummy.

We had 7 precious days together

There was no way I was leaving Brady alone in the hospital. My home for the next 6 nights was Ward 1 at Sheffield Children's Hospital.

I was given a tiny room next to the ward and I was allowed to go and sit next to the incubator for as long as I wanted. Brady was sealed in and given whatever he needed. He was being fed intravenously and he needed help with his breathing.

The six days were long and sleepless. I felt helpless. I was living off food from the vending machine and spent hours walking the corridors. All of our family came to visit. I got to put my hand inside the incubator only once or twice to touch Brady. The hospital didn't want him to suffer any type of infection.

On a few occasions he cried and frowned. His cry was so soft. I cried in unison with him. The nurses looked at me and joined me in my weak moments. It was impossible to avoid.

I made friends with other parents on the ward. There was another baby in special care. He was six months old and had feeding problems. He looked so strong compared to my little Brady.

My big mistake

It was a Sunday and my family had been to visit. There had been no change in Brady's condition, and they suggested I come home to have Sunday tea and go back the next day. I was persuaded to do just that and it's a decision I will live to regret for the rest of my days.

The journey from Sheffield to Renishaw (where I lived at the time) took 30 minutes. The moment I walked through the door, I was greeted with the news that the hospital had telephoned. I rang back immediately.

"You'd better come back Mr Lilley. Brady is struggling."

I ran upstairs and grabbed my bible. I was not and have never really been the deeply religious sort, but I had in my head that people cannot enter into heaven unless they have been Christened. At the time, Brady had not been. The beautiful little fella had been fighting for his life in an incubator. I decided

I was going to try and Christen him myself, just in case. I realise this sounds completely irrational but, in that moment, it's what I wanted to do.

He had passed away

When Julie and I arrived at the ward, we were greeted by sad faces. *"David, I'm really sorry, Brady has passed away."*

With my bible in my hand, I stood by his incubator. The ventilator was still breathing for him, but the alarm was going off constantly. His heart had stopped beating. I read part of *'The Lord is my Shepherd'* from the bible and I broke down.

Julie and I held hands and looked at him. I asked them to please stop the alarm going off. They asked us if we would like to hold Brady. We had not held him at any point during his life. I had gently touched his skin through the incubator but that was all.

The only time we got to hold him

The nurses took us into a side office and 10 minutes later, they brought a tiny bundle through, wrapped in a blanket. The nurse tried to give him to me, but I was a quivering mess. I asked them to give Brady to Julie.

As I write these words, I can see the picture now. It feels like I am back there. I can see Julie's face, what she was wearing, and I can see the tears flowing uncontrollably down her face.

Julie reached the point where she wanted me to hold him. He was so tiny. I stroked his cheek. It was still warm. I kissed him on the head and looked at him, examining his every feature and feeling like I had let him down. We sat in the room for at least an hour. We did not want to let him go. We were asked a question about post-mortems, which we rejected. They took Brady away.

As I walked from the hospital, I went on to the ward where the parents of the other baby were. They stood up. The father stepped forward, hugged me and cried. We held on for a minute. He said he was sorry in my ear. I could not answer him.

The journey home was a quiet one. Not a word was spoken. When we got back to Julie's mum's, Julie's Dad greeted her with a huge hug. I had never seen him cry. He had beautiful eyes. He was a nice man and seeing him hug his own baby, his own blood, was so poignant. He could not talk. None of us could. I just sat and cried. I cried like I have never cried before and I could not summon any thoughts to stop the flow. I have no memories of the next 48 hours, other than receiving a flood of visitors, dozens of sympathy cards and a lot of tears.

The final goodbye

The funeral was quickly planned. We were asked if we wanted to see Brady again before the funeral. I was the only one who felt strong enough to see him.

I can still see him now. People said that it would be my only memory of him, and I should remember him as I had last seen him. I had been with him for a week, no one else had, and I wanted to say one final goodbye.

It was like he was laid in a beautiful cot. Brady had a tiny bonnet on and a cotton blanket. He had a white rose and a small teddy bear that had been given to him. I stayed with him for 15 minutes. I talked to him. I told him that I was sorry, that I loved him and that he would always be with me and I would always be with him, both in my heart and mind. I bent down and carefully kissed his head. I paused at the door as I left. I was a broken young man.

We held a full funeral. Brady's coffin was tiny. I can only remember three things; I remember his tiny coffin being carried in and out of the church, with me and Julie walking with our heads bowed behind. I remember his burial. He rests under an oak tree and his Grandad Brian's ashes are now with him.

Life afterwards

In the weeks that followed the funeral, life was hard. We had such a glaring hole in our life. I sat around and thought of Brady. I was angry with myself for nipping home on that Sunday. I could not figure out what to do with myself. I supported Julie as best as I could, but I wasn't sure what to do or what to say. I didn't have the life experience or maturity to know what to do.

Life now

As I look back over the 31 years that have passed, I can declare that Brady is in my thoughts every day. I feel like he is actually with me.

There are not any easy positives that anyone can draw from this type of experience and I am not going to try to focus too much on that. However, in Brady's memory, I have raised funds for many children's charities. I am actually a co-founder and director of a children's charity and we do what we can to help other families and children.

As I reflect deeper on my experience, I can see how this experience creates more of a respect for time. Brady only had 7 precious days of life.

Those of us who live long lives are fortunate. Those who

steer clear of illness and adversity are very lucky. Gratitude is something we should all have for any fortune that comes our way. Fortune does not come in the shape of money. I feel it comes in the shape of time, health, empathy, love, kindness, humility, understanding and making memories. I refer to this as THELKHUM and it's something you can read about via Google and on Free Podcasts.

Respect for time

Time has become something that I have huge respect for. I manage my time and invest it with care. I spend it with people who I like and respect, or on those who need it. I use some of my time to help others.

In almost all instances, I don't ask for anything in return for my time. Some people are hugely grateful for my time and support and some take me for granted. It's just life. But I get satisfaction from giving and it's what I seek – the feeling of knowing I have helped someone. It's enough.

Empathy

I have concluded that anyone who has suffered in the way that we did with Brady, is likely to develop a quality of empathy and that of a deep caring for others. If there is one positive that I can point to, this is it. Brady's legacy is that his old man is empathetic, has a good heart and tries to help people.

If the world had more empathetic people, there would be no wars, less acrimony and our planet would be a better place to live. Taking some time to study and practice empathy is a good recommendation.

My message to you

If you are reading this to help you overcome your own birth trauma, please know that your pain will subside, and your life can go on positively. It won't feel like this now but each day the pain fades to a bearable level. The memories will always be there, but you have a life to live and be grateful for every healthy moment you get to enjoy. My heart reaches out to you. Please know that people care for you more than words can describe.

Brady now has a brother and three sisters. I am married to Sarah, a person I love more than she could ever know.

Julie is happily married to a fine man.

***

David Lilley is a vastly experienced marketing & business development consultant from Derbyshire in the United Kingdom. With a career that has spanned three decades, David has worked for and alongside several blue-chip brands. This includes the likes of American Experience, Hiscox Insurance, Barclays, Mastercard, Wyndham, Hotels BT & British Gas to name just a few.

David remains a sought-after business development consultant and has built a reputation as a man who can effectively combine modern marketing channels and techniques with strong logic, whilst understanding and harnessing basic human psychology.

A father to five children and having endured a troubled childhood, David has developed an infatuation with the study of human happiness, life progress & contentment. He is the creator of the Thelkhum formula and a regular practitioner of various types of philanthropy. David links some of his characteristics back to the sad baby trauma experience he endured in the 1980s, a story he shares inside the pages of this book.

https://thelkhum.com/
https://uniquenet.co.uk/

Jackie

Positive Birth

Is it even possible to plan for a positive birth?

In my opinion... Yes, it is.

PTSD can happen to any one of us. When something traumatic happens, an internal protective alarm is raised in our unconscious mind, causing physiological and emotional responses.

I feel very privileged to have been asked to contribute to a book giving women a platform from which to tell their own story of birth trauma; it is a subject that until recently was not even recognised, and post-traumatic stress disorder (PTSD) was a diagnosis given to troops returning from war zones not women having babies.

'When something traumatic happens in your life it rocks you to the core. The world is no longer a safe place. It becomes somewhere that bad things can and do happen' – (Mind.co.uk)

The problem with PTSD, is that the alarm continues, and the unpleasant feelings associated with the original event, can be re-experienced if anything happens that is emotionally reminiscent of it.

The Birth Trauma Association (BTA) suggest that 30,000 women a year experience birth trauma with ongoing symptoms such as flashbacks, anxiety, hyper-vigilance and avoidance of anything that brings back memories of their birth (Birthtraumaassociation.org.uk).

Healthcare professionals and wider society need to hear the voices of the contributors in this book in order to break the taboo surrounding the subject; PTSD due to birth experience exists and the sooner we all acknowledge the elephant in the room, the sooner we can tackle it head on and begin to heal the families who are left to deal with the consequences. I have been asked to provide some pointers to help negotiate a pregnancy in the direction of a confidence-filled birth experience and will do this to the best of my ability but cannot (of course) guarantee perfection; life-changing, transformational journeys in life – being born, giving birth and dying – are supremely individual, and experience of them is complex and infinitely variable… and in my mind, rightly so.

I am a Certified Birth Trauma Resolution Practitioner, and have seen approximately 60 women over the past 2 years, talking and listening to their stories and offering them techniques that work in order that they can feel free of the troublesome symptoms that remain after a traumatic birth, not by erasing the memory, but by removing some of the debilitating weight that attaches itself to those memories causing negative issues weeks, months and years later.

Interestingly, some of those women have been colleagues affected by their own or others' births, and worried about being able to cope in their roles as professionals. I am regularly moved to tears by the words I hear and the resilience of those recounting the tales in such amazing detail – often several years after the event.

I think it is necessary to reveal now that I, like every other author in this book experienced trauma giving birth. My trauma wasn't due to issues at the time, but of ingrained memories of childhood sexual abuse that flooded to the surface and became tangled up in the whole experience causing horribly frightening and intense flashbacks at the time and for many years afterwards. I thought I had buried these memories deeply, so deeply that I had almost forgotten about them because I had moved on in life: I was about to have my first baby and having read and re-read Miriam Stoppard's pregnancy book, felt I was ready for anything and everything. I was fully prepared, I knew (via Miriam's descriptions) what to expect and to the outside world everything appeared to be fine, but I was battling internal mind-demons, experiencing constant self-talk prior to and during any meeting with Midwives or Obstetricians, mentally working incredibly hard to show how wonderfully well I was coping. I was very quiet in labour, making my internal distress invisible, effectively disappearing inside myself whilst I dealt with the battles going on in my head. I later found out that this was called 'dissociation' and still catch myself dropping into this state at times when I'm feeling overwhelmed or frightened during intense situations.

The gaps I have in the memories around this time held me captive for many years, but the fascination I have around the mind and emotions during pregnancy and birth sent me on my trajectory in life, I became a Midwife… … Someone who would stand with women during labour, lending strength, maintaining safety, hearing rather than just listening and mostly… being kind.

I share absolute, unconditional love with everyone who has a birth story to tell, you are all awesome in my eyes x

As a practicing Midwife, I am privileged to hear birth stories on a daily basis, the majority of them are told with beaming smiles and shining eyes. Some, however, leave me feeling uneasy and with far more questions than answers. I am also a holistic practitioner and possess a more alternative, spiritual mindset with fundamental beliefs in our innate mind/body powers and the unmeasurable forces around us. I'm constantly in awe of humankind, of the power we hold inside us, and the way natural processes unfold when they are supported, nurtured and unhurried.

Trauma is a subjective concept; and trauma around birth is no exception. What one person deems a traumatic experience might appear very differently to someone else. A 'normal, straightforward birth' to a midwife or obstetrician can be experienced and indeed described as something totally different by a new parent – humans are wonderfully complicated, and non-judgmental listening is required in order to really hear what is and *isn't* being said.

Birth is often described as a 'rite of passage' a point at which a new life chapter begins.

Preparing for this monumental change is a very personal choice, dependent on a variety of factors.

The issue of personal choice is very important but is dependent on parents-to-be having the motivation to research for themselves or being given the information they need by someone with the time and the knowledge. There is a never-ending supply of information available at the touch of a button, however most of it is unregulated and is often conflicting. Sometimes, I feel dismayed at how little actual preparation is made when a baby is expected. A LOT of expensive 'stuff' is bought, but the time spent in preparation rarely equates to the money spent on equipment. For example, if you were about to get married or go on honeymoon, or have decided to splash out on a really expensive holiday, it's likely you'll want to 'plan' for it in quite some detail; it's an important time in your life, you're making memories and probably spending a large amount of money too. Researching the vast wealth of information to help you make decisions about probably THE most important life change you're ever likely to experience, will be worth the time and effort. I cannot guarantee that by following the suggestions in this chapter that you will achieve perfection during pregnancy, birth and parenthood, that would be utterly ridiculous. There will be twists and turns along the way that change the direction of your journey for a while or affect the eventual outcome, it is part of life, and life is unpredictable in nature.

Is it possible to plan ahead when you're pregnant?

In my opinion, yes.

I thought about a mnemonic to act as a guide ('POWERS') which could be used as a starting point when deciding how to negotiate the confusing world of maternity care. This list is by no means exhaustive but could be useful for exploring ideas in your own geographical area.

Becoming connected with your body and your developing baby, investing some time and energy into preparing for this momentous event and truly investigating all the options that appeal to you as an individual will pay off in the long run. Remember the saying "knowledge is power"; in this case it is very true.

I have put this list together drawing from many years of experience working in the NHS maternity services and being self-employed too, speaking with other midwives and healthcare practitioners as well as many passionate, knowledgeable mums, dads and service providers and I, like everyone in the UK, am a lifelong advocate for the principles of the NHS system of care, however I am a realist and accept that resources within it are finite. Many of the services, groups and sessions available during pregnancy, birth and afterwards, cost money. However, there are a great many 'taster' and 'free initial' sessions available plus reduced rates for anyone on low incomes and anyone who is authentic will always be willing to have an initial conversation, so you can get a feel for what it is they are offering. I will add here though, it is really important to research an individual's qualifications and philosophies, ideally through direct contact or word-of-mouth recommendation.

Having a baby, whether it's your first or your fifth is monumental, it's life changing and 'going with the flow' is fine to an extent but knowledge is powerful and you need to feel powerful when you bring new life into the world.

POWERS

P is for 'Positivity' – possessing a generally optimistic outlook on your pregnancy and upcoming birth might sound a little trite, I certainly don't mean it to! Surrounding yourself with people who lift your spirits and fill your ears with positivity and strength means that your attitude to the future – your pregnancy, birth and parenthood, change subtly. Incremental changes grow larger further down the line and the ripples often spread outwards into other areas of life, magically over time. Becoming pregnant is the perfect opportunity to start regarding your body with the awe it deserves. It is doing exactly what it needs to do, even if you have had help getting pregnant initially, or you are being supported by specialist services – your amazing human body carries out countless complex processes to keep everything in balance.

As little girls, we learn the value we place on our body by watching and listening to those closest to us – our parents, siblings and wider family members. As we get older, our friendship groups and the media also influence that belief system. Put simply, these early developmental influences can strengthen positive or negative attitudes to our bodies which affect mindset further along the line. Becoming pregnant may be the perfect opportunity to write a whole new chapter, the turning point where real change can begin. Preparing to give birth with a positive mental attitude is allowing the opening of a door into new experiences that offers a change of mindset, for growth in another direction and that is why positivity is important – it drives you forward in search of what is right for you as an individual.

O is for 'Organisation' – being organised really pays off down the line. Preparation and planning are key. You don't have to be a certain 'type' to benefit from exploring the variety of options available to you during pregnancy, birth and as new parents, nor do you have to be labelled as 'low risk', in fact, planning and organisation when a pregnancy is more complicated can help you and your caregivers individualise your care, placing focus on you and your baby rather than the system – make the maternity organisation work for you. Many strategies are available online for free or very little financial outlay, self-help books can be borrowed from the library, asking friends and family what they found useful or helpful is a good starting point.

You don't have to be a hippie to find value in strategies such as hypnobirthing or pregnancy yoga, both teach relaxation skills that are supported by an abundance of evidence and are beneficial in the pregnancy period and for life. Keeping physically active with activities such as swimming or walking regularly reduces the aches and niggles many women experience and being organised with exercise helps baby into an optimal position towards the end of pregnancy too. Indeed, regular exercise such as walking in nature has proven benefits to mental health (mind.org)

Considering your birth preferences (birth plan) makes good organisational sense and these can be discussed with your community midwife at one of your regular appointments.

There are thousands of templates available online that you can download or use as a point of reference. As well as written birth preference templates, there are some great image-based 'visual birth plans' available online to download and print off. You cannot 'plan' for the birth you want because birth, like life, can be unpredictable, but thinking about the aspects of care that are important to you and recording them in an organised way makes great sense.

W is for 'Wisdom' – like it or not, believe it or not, we all possess an inner wisdom. A little internal voice that gives us the answers to our questions should we choose to listen, it is linked to 'gut instinct' and is based in belief rather than evidence. Spiritually, it might be called the 'higher self' or 'higher power' or perhaps 'intuition'.

Spending quiet time, listening to our thoughts, connecting to our baby on an intuitive level is a healthy habit to cultivate whilst pregnant. Becoming self-aware is a hot topic currently and it feels to me like the worm is turning at last, many people are realising that there is a benefit in spending time focusing inward, tuning in to the way we think, act and react to life. Pregnancy is traditionally viewed as a rite of passage, an opportunity to open the mind and widen horizons, to appreciate our incredibly complicated, amazing mind and body, re-evaluating our present and future... ...Wow!

E is for 'Environment' – it is a fact that place of birth impacts on birth experience and whether you are considered high or low risk, I cannot emphasize enough the importance of considering *where* to have your baby. I could write a whole book based around birth environment but will provide a short guide here.

There are a variety of settings available depending on where you live and as a home-birth team midwife, I support women in their own homes but have experience in a variety of settings. However, there are situations where having a baby at home is not sensible, advisable or indeed desired by parents. As a midwife, I support and advocate for choice and as previously mentioned you cannot make a choice if you are unaware you have choices. Generally, though, homebirth, birth centre or hospital are the 3 environmental areas available. Your community midwife will know about you as an individual, your past medical and surgical history, your pregnancy history and personal preferences so is ideally placed to discuss this with you. Remember though, birth environment – *where* you give birth is your decision and healthcare professionals are your guides, providing information from which YOU make the choice.

As mammals, we labour and birth with certain processes taking place. If you watch any mammal giving birth, it is done with instinct and this subtle innate behaviour works best when there is a feeling of safety and the freedom to just 'go with it'. Please do not think that if you're considered 'high risk' that this means you have no choice of birth environment, you absolutely do. With a little pre-planning and good midwifery and obstetric support, it is possible to make adjustments that can help you feel more comfortable, supporting instinctive behaviour and maintaining safety. The following list gives some suggestions to consider, adapted from some insightful work undertaken in 2013*:

Privacy – giving birth is a series of processes and involves intimate parts of our body, feeling observed or being disturbed will inhibit those subtle, hormonally driven processes.

Lighting – dimming the lights or turning them off, using a lamp or cot heater light instead as light affects the delicate hormonal release of oxytocin, melatonin and endorphins.

Water – the use of water during labour and birth has been

acknowledged as beneficial for decades and having access to a bath or pool benefits all women who choose this option. Most maternity units have telemetry monitors available if you require continuous electronic monitoring during labour and this option can be discussed and planned beforehand.

Support – birth partner support is crucial. Your birth partner or partners are there to lend you strength and encouragement, it is a complete privilege to be present at the birth of another human and excellent support makes a massive difference. Birth partner support will be discussed in more detail later.

*'Birthspace' also discusses the bed, decor, furniture and equipment, available space to move around, inclusion of nature, smells, en-suite bathroom, windows and noise.
*Jenkinson, B., Josey, N., & Kruske, S. (2013) 'BirthSpace: An evidence-based guide to birth environment design' Queensland Centre for Mothers & Babies, The University of Queensland. https//:espace.library.uq.edu.au

R is for 'R-E-L-A-X' – whatever it takes for you to be relaxed… then do that!

Gather together everything you need; tools and techniques, knowledge, distractions, people and strategies that you can rely on. This is YOUR time, YOUR experience and it's important for you to feel calm and relaxed throughout, flowing with the sensations of birth, having the knowledge that you can bend, rather than break should a situation change. It takes preparation and practice to relax with purpose, to breathe slowly in….and even more slowly out to engage the para-sympathetic nervous system, slowing the heart rate and allowing birth hormones to flow without hindrance.

Perhaps visualisation is something you might like to try – imagining yourself being in a bubble of light, a barrier where everything inside is safe and calm. Relaxation is a skill and it takes practice to develop the ability to relax. We seem to have lost our way as far as focusing on 'being' rather than 'doing' but there are literally thousands of guided visualisations available for free online and all they require is an open mind. Relaxing into the journey and being in the moment is key.

S is for 'Support' – the person or people who are with you during your birth can positively or negatively impact upon the way your mind and body act and react to the twists and turns of labour and birth. Your partner, mum, sister or best friend (usually a female but there's no reason why you couldn't have a male) or perhaps you want to employ a private doula – these are all choices for you. The physical, emotional and even spiritual presence of someone who knows you and knows your wishes, who can lend strength and really tune-in to you as you labour, is invaluable. Your midwife will very quickly tune in to you as an individual and work with you and your birth partner(s) as a team, explaining everything, facilitating choice and lending strength and knowledge. Your support team need to know what to expect as they will be your voice when you need one. Going along to birth preparation classes with your birth partner/ support person is one way of preparing together. Make sure you get what YOU need from any sessions, they are not all the same so ask around and see what others recommend, contact and speak to whoever facilitates the sessions and get a feel for them and the way they work.

Your midwife is an invaluable support and will be the healthcare professional providing your care however or wherever you have your baby. He/she is a specialist in normality and will only refer to an obstetrician when something is out of the normal range, acting as your advocate if you need one. It's important to gather support for afterwards too, having practical help to transition in the early days as a family is a real bonus. Tip – don't turn down offers of help too many times as people will stop offering! The support of those nearest to you is invaluable, never be afraid or embarrassed to ask for help.

How can birth lead to PTSD?

Similar physiological processes are inherent in all mammalian births, but individual experience is dependent on a hundred variables that come together at any particular moment, at that particular time. The way a woman is treated during her pregnancy, birth and afterwards is down to the people involved in her care. In my experience, everything boils down to the way she and her partner are made to feel at any point in the process. Individual thoughts and feelings are subjective in nature – open to interpretation, misinterpretation and misunderstanding. Human beings are on the whole unpredictable and superbly complicated.

I will briefly summarise some of the main situations that appear to have contributed to a diagnosis of PTSD from the birth stories I have heard as a BTR practitioner.

Emergencies – there are rare occasions when suddenly something happens, and an emergency situation arises; a series of actions ensue which can leave women and their birth partners with traumatic memories of the event. It is easy for all concerned to understand that thorough debriefing and aftercare are needed and provided as a matter of course and the experience is then usually integrated into the unconscious mind once understanding has been reached.

Communication and interaction – language used, tone of

voice, manner and body language can all have a profound impact on confidence and trust in both positive and negative ways; words are powerful when emotions are on the surface and having a baby is an intensely emotive time. Emotions cause changes in body chemistry, so words and language are powerful tools that can uplift and empower or totally render the recipient disempowered and defeated.

Control – the women I speak to about birth, about their overall thoughts hopes and memories, will invariably mention the word 'control' – feeling in control, feeling out of control, having no control. Hindsight enables a review of an experience with the luxury of time and distance and often the negative emotions associated with that experience are the ones that rise to the top, leaving feelings of anger, anxiety, disappointment and fear. However, the feeling of being in or out of control, is a thread that runs through all the stories I have heard. As a Midwife, it is important to acknowledge and respect this need at all times and to facilitate every woman's right to feel and experience personal control.

Coercion – many women feel that they have no choice but to accept what they are told. Emotive words such as 'risk' and 'stillbirth' are peppered into conversations about plans of care and women do not want to risk harm coming to their babies. Induction of labour is by far the most common situation where women I have spoken to feel they have no choice but to accept intervention.

Unrealised expectations – i.e. the plan did not go to plan. Situations where the outcome was in direct opposition to the intention, such as a planned home birth ending in a transfer to hospital, labouring in the pool at the birth centre changed to having an emergency caesarian section. Assisted births (forceps or ventouse) could also be included here, together with having stitches, infection in labour or perhaps needing to go to theatre. These sorts of circumstances may well have been absolutely necessary but as we know, memories get mixed in with perception and understanding of events at the time. It is rarely black and white but a variety of shades of grey.

The cascade of intervention – is a long-accepted concept which suggests that once an intervention occurs, more follow as normal birth physiology has been interrupted. It is similar to a domino-effect, once one is knocked down the others follow.

Unexpected outcomes – I am referring to mum or baby being sick, injured or dying. Sensitive, specialised and individualised care would always be offered in these instances as well as referral to appropriate support services.

Treatment for PTSD

The first and hardest part of having a traumatic birth, is recognising the fact.

Bringing new life into the world takes grit and determination, it demands a woman to acknowledge her 'self', her very being in the deepest most profound way and takes her physically, emotionally and spiritually to places she has never been before. It can be scary, exciting and unpredictable but ultimately it should lead to growth and positive change for parents. The first few days after having a baby is likely to be a natural period of reflection, as the mind, body and soul process and adjust to this new situation. Communicating with midwives and loved ones about how you 'feel' at this time is vital to gain objective feedback on the experience, increase understanding and begin to settle into a new role as a parent, no matter which number baby this is; each birth is individual.

It is normal and healthy during these early days to remember snippets of the birth and things that were said and done. In my experience there may be transient forgetfulness, but memory tends to return gently and naturally over the following days and weeks. Women who are struggling to process the experience have blank spaces several days and weeks afterwards, often long periods of time where they have no recollection at all of what happened. A session with a healthcare professional who can go through the notes can be beneficial in this instance and sometimes, this 'filling in the blanks' is all that is needed. If the memories of birth are distressing, causing bad dreams, flashbacks, anger and deep sadness – it is vitally important to seek help sooner rather than later. Yes, time is a healer but being pro-active where there is PTSD will speed up the healing process.

The first contact is likely to be with your GP who can refer and signpost to relevant services.

The National Institute for Clinical Excellence (NICE) Guidelines recommends Cognitive Behavioural Therapy (CBT) and Eye Movement Desensitisation and Reprocessing (EMDR) for the treatment of PTSD (nice.org.uk NG116). Referral to services is via a medical professional, waiting lists are lengthy on the NHS but these treatments are readily available privately.

Some trusts have a specialist maternity team who provide clinical support for women with underlying mental health issues, severe fear of birth (tocophobia or tokophobia) or PTSD due to a previous birth experience and require referral from your midwife or GP.

Most maternity departments offer a debriefing service for anyone wanting to talk about their birth experience with the benefit of being able to refer to the written notes that were taken at the time. Many couples find this a useful starting point, as a discussion with the notes can fill in many of the blanks that exist for parents and birth partners.

Hospital notes can be requested and photocopied for a fee by applying to the Medical Records Manager at your trust.

I personally provide a hypnotherapy-based treatment called 'Certified Birth Trauma Resolution' (BTR) and highly qualified practitioners can be contacted via www.birthtraumaresolution.org many of whom are healthcare professionals themselves.

Hypno-therapeutic techniques used during BTR work very effectively, often with a single session and provide tools for relaxation that can be used and developed further. I also offer a 'positive birth rehearsal' under hypnosis for anyone who is expecting a baby after the initial BTR session. I cannot describe how effective and life-changing this simple therapy is. It led to further training and qualification as a Hypnotherapist and Mind Coach.

Hypnosis, however, is not recommended by NICE but is another avenue for exploration and opportunity for choice.

I am more than happy to be contacted for information and advice on appropriate treatment options.

I know that the initial contact is hard but promise that it is the first step in healing the pain and the past.

★★★

Jackie Allatson works part-time as an NHS home birth team Midwife in Leicestershire and is also a Holistic and Hypno-therapist working from home. She qualified as a Certified Birth Trauma Resolution Practitioner in 2017 and regularly sees and treats parents and members of staff who are struggling due to negative experiences or fears around birth. She is fascinated with the power of the mind and seeks out alternative ways of thinking and being whenever possible!

Jackie also loves teaching and runs birth preparation classes both for the NHS and privately as 'Down to Earth Jackie'. She is a mum of three beautiful grown-up children and the four most perfect grandchildren.

Jackie is based near Melton Mowbray, Leicestershire, and can be contacted via her website:

www.downtoearthjackie.co.uk

Email: downtoearthjackie@gmail.com

Jackie is available on Facebook and Instagram, search for 'Down To Earth Jackie'.

Words of Wisdom

Words of guidance, support, advice, hope and encouragement from mums who have already walked a mile in your shoes.

"After you have your precious baby your thoughts may turn to wanting to get rid of the baby weight. You may be unhappy with the way you look or how your body now feels. I ask that you are kind to yourself, that you remember the amazing transformation your body has been through as it grew and nurtured your precious bundle. Try to love yourself as you are."
– Laura Bland, mum to Callie

"It's ok to be tired, it's ok to not feel yourself, it's very normal to feel like you're not being the best parent. Accept the help from others, sleep when you can & always know you're not alone! You are amazing and you are being a fantastic parent! This is the most rewarding gift you've ever given, the gift of life x."
– Laura Young, mum to Dylan and Ethan

"Giving birth is a beautiful and traumatic experience, your body just went through so much. Motherhood isn't easy; it's beautiful but it also has so many challenges – YOU have got this! Rest! Ask for help when you need it! Love yourself! Take five minutes when you have to. And listen to your gut rather than what others say – Mama knows best!"
– Mo Frances, mum to Rachel, Joshua and Elizabeth

"Using a baby carrier or sling can be a brilliant way to bond with your baby. When used safely and fitted correctly, they can be worn for as long as you and your baby are happy. Slings can help reduce crying, colic, improve communication, reduce isolation in caregiver and even be used in exercise. Please see your local sling library who can help you choose the right sling for you."

– Rachel Devereux, mum to Caeleb and Hemera

"Nobody prepared me for the changes my body was going through during postpartum, if I could give any new mama some advice, it would be... What your body is going through is completely natural, you are not alone. Be kinder to yourself, you have been through a lot, you are stronger than you think. Find gratitude for what your body has given you and survived. Time is so precious, don't waste it. YOU are sensational!"

– Ana Louise Bonasera, mum to Nathaniel, Jude, Luca and Spencer

"Trust in your instincts. Don't wish time away, before long, this brand-new baby who won't stop crying and eating will be seventeen, and won't stop whinging and eating, except you won't get the midnight cuddles, eyes that look into your soul and endless kisses! Most of all, there isn't such a thing as a 'right' way, your way is the best way!"

– Louise Caunce, mum to Ryan, Ray and Robyn

"Absolutely ask for help! If you can afford to, invest in a doula. Even just for a few hours here and there. You are never alone, and you don't have to feel alone. Please reach out, there are many services able to support you, however you may need it."

– Liz Haynes, mum to Alanna

"There's no such thing as a perfect parent, and mums in particular are set up to fail. Every time you hold your beautiful baby, it's a win. Every time you meet their gaze with unconditional love, they grow because you did. They don't care how you look, just how you make them feel, so hold them, look into their eyes and know you are good enough, because they know it already."

– Katherine Bellchambers-Wilson, mum to Jacob and Joel

"You've got this! Yes, that's right, that's all I need to say to you; you've got this. What's that? You feel exhausted? Everybody is giving you opinions? Ignore them. This is you, this is your child, this is your time. Everybody has an opinion, they're like arseholes. You don't need to do what anyone else is doing, you need to do what's right for you. If you need help, you're not alone. If you're offered help, take it. You've got this!"

– Laura Jane Dernie, mum to Jack and Poppy

"Dear new mum,

Be kind.

You're both still learning, so be kind to yourself and your little one.

Be now.

Try to stay in the moment as much as possible. Fully experience both the good and the bad, because whatever it is, it will eventually pass.

Be you.

Your baby doesn't need perfection she just needs you – the perfectly imperfect you."

– Angharad Davis, mum to Owen and Mateo

"Throw away the rulebook... not that there is one. Just love unconditionally, and it's ok to get it wrong sometimes."

– Lisa Haines, mum to Natasha

"To the Mum whose baby never took a breath.
How did I cope? One day at a time, I allowed myself time to accept what I had no control over. I told myself that from that moment forward I would always live life to the fullest, make magical memories with your siblings that you would never have the opportunity to experience. You are the reason that your siblings have a wonderful childhood. Your loss became a positive, it had to have happened for a reason otherwise I would have just given up. You drive me in everything I do and every goal I set is because you didn't get a chance. You only knew love."

– Jessica Tyrell, mum to Noah, Ava and Elsie

"Take a note of how you're feeling, good days and bad. Talk! Talk to your GP, your health visitor, your social worker, your mum, your best friend, your sister, your aunty – anyone! Take the offer of help, whether it be having a 10-minute bath while someone watches the baby. Take the time to heal, mentally and physically – you'll never get back to "normal" because it doesn't exist anymore!"

– Louise Clatworthy, mum to Grace and Lily

"Try not to expect too much of yourself. You're adjusting and learning about how to be a parent. It takes time and is not something that happens overnight.
Try and get help from family and friends so they can do some cleaning, cooking and shopping, whilst you rest whenever you can, so you can spend time getting to know your baby and vice versa. You'll never get that time back and it's so precious. From strong foundations will grow great relationships."

– Anita Hill, mum to Bea and Flo

"I still struggle with GUILT!
Feeling guilty …

- For not wanting visitors in the first few months.
- That I let them come anyway and struggled with breastfeeding as a result.
- That I ended up bottle feeding my first and not trying harder.
- When people passed my baby around a room of strangers; I should be protecting him.
- For having to send my son to nursery when he was so sad to leave me!"

– Natalie Kyne-Dinsdale, mum to Finn and Orla

"We can't stop ourselves from feeling overwhelmed, angry or hurt. These are normal emotions. They show us that something isn't right and that we need to look deeper to what that emotion is trying to tell us. Only from there can we then find our way out and learn to help ourselves and in turn show our children what strength is. We are strong, we just need to remember there is always a way through."

– Alexandra Kremer, mum to Rufus and Eden

"To the new Mum: Your body has gone through a massive change from pregnancy to having a baby!
Your hormones are adjusting, your body is recovering, and you are most probably sleep deprived!
Please be kind on yourself! You are doing a great job! Both you and your baby are learning new skills and finding your feet.
Don't be afraid to ask for help if you need it and don't feel guilty about turning visitors away."

– Kate Hancox, mum to Jamie and Leo

"Losing a child at birth has got to be one of the hardest things anyone ever goes through. It is a grief that overwhelms the parent. Things improved for me when I came across an article that mentioned a culture that mourned a birth. They saw it as the trapping of a soul, in a physical body, and that death was a chance to celebrate the soul being released to go wherever it desired."

– Joy Gill, mum to Holli (rainbow baby 6 years later)

"Here's a thing people don't tell you about being a parent: none of us know what we're doing. We all make it up as we go along. You're never going to be a perfect parent… and that's OK. None of us are. And you don't need to be perfect: a 'good enough parent' is good enough! And you are good enough, even when you think you're not."

– Lizi Jackson-Barrett, mum to Jacob and Layla

"You cannot spoil a baby. There is no such thing as a rod for your back. You will never look back and wish you had held your baby less. Babies need to be near to you to feel safe. They cannot sleep if they do not feel safe. Your baby is not the only one who refuses to stay asleep in their cot!"

– Hannah, mum to Poppy and Bess

"Parenting is all about survival, yours and theirs. Whatever it takes to get through the day. Some days that will mean TVs, tablets and processed food. Don't feel bad. As long as everyone goes to bed fed and ok then you've done well. Everyday can't be parks and homemade food; we're all doing the best we can and it's not a competition."

– Karen, mum to Madeleine, Hugo,
Beatrice and Claudia

"All around you it may seem, other parents living the dream. You may feel you are struggling along, please listen to your inner song. In my experience everyone is making it up as they go along. Just follow your instincts and stay strong."
– Anne Rees, mother to Ezra

"I had a traumatic birth, which not only was hard on me, it also had a huge impact on my husband. I remember when I was pregnant, my mum advising me to always look out for each other, as once your little one grows up, it'll just be the two of you. That advice has also helped my daughter to see how to treat others and the bond that the three of us have is so strong."
– Claire Clements, mum to Ellie

"Parenting is, without a doubt, the most paradoxical experience you'll ever have. One minute you're gushing with overwhelming love after a flash of toothpaste smile, the next you're wishing you're on another planet so somebody else can take over. It's all normal. Allow yourself to feel the full spectrum because that's what it is to embrace parenthood. Be with it. Be in it. Be you."
– Abi Yardimci, mum to Baran and Azad

"When everything seems dark and hope is fading you must find your light. Your light is all that powers you. Sometimes others will help you light up and that's ok too; seek the help and allow others in. You are never alone in your pain, whatever may have caused it. Shine bright, keep the hope and love flowing and always remember your never alone."
– Eliz Jedras, mum to Ruby, Phoenix,
and bump due March 2020

"You are unique and so is your baby. You can listen to advice but trust your instincts. If it feels right or wrong, it probably is. You can only do what feels right for your family in that moment, without guilt or explanation. Times change, advice evolves, but this is your time and your choice."

– Emma Goodburn, mum to Poppy, Beth and Phoebe

Support

Pandas Foundation

Mental health support, advice and guidance for parents experiencing peri-natal struggle.
www.pandasfoundation.org.uk

MIND

Advice and support to empower anyone experiencing a mental health problem, including birth trauma or birth related PTSD.
www.mind.org.uk

Sands (Stillbirth & Neonatal Death Charity)

Sands exists to ensure that anyone affected by the death of a baby receives the best possible care and support for as long as they need it wherever they are in the UK.
www.sands.org.uk

For Counselling

To find a counsellor, visit the British Association for Counselling and Psychotherapy
www.bacp.co.uk

Printed in Great Britain
by Amazon

43705535R00129